Praise for medici

We have been waiting for a book like this for years. A straight-forward guide, without ego, lengthy case studies, drama or diversions to how you can perform shamanic healings without spending years in a jungle or working on thousands of clients – because the author has already done it for you. This is the only book on shamanic healing you will ever need. Five stars *****
Tania Ahsan, Editor *Kindred Spirit* **magazine**

I have really enjoyed this apprenticeship. My life has trans-formed and I have the beginnings of a deeper and more profound self-understanding and a deepened respect for spirit. My complementary therapies have all benefited and I have begun to give treatments of an overtly shamanic nature.
Debbie (San Francisco, USA)

I have great enthusiasm for this course and it has brought all of my previous work (with shamanism as well as my therapy training) into line.
Mark (Devon, UK)

I feel so much better for having done this powerful work; I am in a difficult transition in my life and this will be a great foundation.
Liz (Berlin, Germany)

I am really enjoying the course! It is all that I hoped it would be. It is challenging my world view and I am enjoying the transfor-mation.
Richard (Athens, Greece)

I have found this course rewarding, it has given me the opportunity to explore avenues which I haven't had time in the past to do. It has been good to focus and realize that it's the simple things we do in life which have the most profound effect. Compassion for others and generosity of spirit, things which are so needed in our chaotic society which seems so out of balance.

Robert (Atlanta, US)

Thank you for offering this opportunity. Living where I do, opportunities such as these are not common. It is much appreciated.

Peter (Galway, Ireland)

Medicine for the Soul

The Complete Book of
Shamanic Healing
The Heaven Method™

Medicine for the Soul

The Complete Book of
Shamanic Healing
The Heaven Method™

Ross Heaven

MOON
BOOKS

Winchester, UK
Washington, USA

First published by Moon Books, 2012
Moon Books is an imprint of John Hunt Publishing Ltd., Laurel House, Station Approach,
Alresford, Hants, SO24 9JH, UK
office1@o-books.net
www.o-books.com

For distributor details and how to order please visit the 'Ordering' section on our website.

Text copyright: Ross Heaven 2011

ISBN: 978 1 78099 419 2

A CIP catalogue record for this book is available from the British Library.

Design: Stuart Davies

Printed and bound by CPI Group (UK) Ltd, Croydon, CR0 4YY

We operate a distinctive and ethical publishing philosophy in all
areas of our business, from our global network of authors to
production and worldwide distribution.

CONTENTS

Dedication

This is for the Sarah I knew; the one I read to, who played in our garden, rubbed mud on her face at the waterfall and made beautiful mosaics. *Amor para siempre, fumar y agua.* Rest in peace.

And for my children.

Introduction

Welcome to this book, a complete introduction to shamanic healing. In it you will learn how to journey in the worlds of the shaman to meet spirit guides and allies, how to retrieve power for yourself and others, how to heal shamanically, retrieve lost soul parts, remove spirit intrusions, rebalance the body's energy system and gain guidance for the future using divinatory techniques so you can provide counselling to clients from spirit. Each chapter is a self-contained look at a particular healing theme and includes exercises so you can put your knowledge into practice and begin working with guides and allies. We also look at some of the specialist skills of the shaman such as his work with plant medicines and there will be baths, oils, mixtures and charms you can make for yourself or to help clients.

At the end you will be able to carry out healings for yourself and others and you also have an opportunity to gain a qualification in shamanic healing (The Four Gates *Medicine for the Soul* Diploma in Shamanic Studies) and add your name to our list of recommended healers for client referrals.

The Four Gates is one of Europe's best-known shamanic training organisations. I founded it more than a decade ago and it now has students and healers worldwide who have completed this Diploma.

I have been a shamanic healer, therapist and workshop leader for more than 20 years although my own training began as a child through a chance encounter with a healer and herbalist in a remote English village (a story told in my book *The Sin Eater's Last Confessions*). After studying with him for 10 years and then completing a degree in anthropology, psychology and philosophy I sought out other shamans and healers to learn from in Europe, Haiti, the Amazon rainforest and the Andes of Peru. I have written extensively about these encounters and trainings, including more than 10 books on shamanism and healing. *Medicine for the Soul* is a distillation of this work, providing you with a step-by-step guide to the core essence of what shamans do and how they heal.

There is no 'floweriness' to it, no lengthy case studies and no theorising or speculation. Instead it provides a clear guide, often in simple bulletpoints, to what you do to remove illnesses from clients and restore their power and spirit. Of course, this is a framework and over time and with practice you will adapt it to your own needs and those of your clients but if you follow this framework now there is no reason why you should not be conducting healings by the end of this book.

The *Medicine for the Soul* Diploma in shamanism

In traditional societies shamans do not study for Diplomas. Like other 'tradespeople' their skills are developed through apprenticeships where they work with older and more established healers, a process which can take many years and like any apprenticeship, begins with menial tasks before they are taught much at all or perform healings of their own. Apprenticeships like these are not structured and, depending on the teacher, the shaman-to-be may not actually learn very much or very quickly. A shaman I know in Peru for example trained for more than six years with his teacher before he even led his first ceremony. During this time his mentor did not offer him tuition (for example, explanations of the shamanic cosmology, the energy body or the means by which the soul can be returned); he had to discover it all for himself by observing his teacher as he performed healings for clients. At the end of six years there are still gaps in his knowledge as he is the first to admit.

This book can therefore be regarded as a 'fast-track apprenticeship' and a more comprehensive and faster route to knowledge than traditional methods of learning. Unlike the case of the jungle shaman I mentioned for example, explanations *are* given so you gain the knowledge you need – the background that he currently still lacks but which all shamans must eventually accumulate. Through practice you will also apply this knowledge by working with others and seeing the results of your healings. *Your* apprenticeship takes weeks rather than years. It will still require dedication on your part however.

The modern Western world is not the Amazon rainforest and unlike traditional shamanic cultures there is one thing that our clients often demand – and that is proof. A qualification is evidence of your claims as a healer. It affirms your dedication to the art of healing and confirms that you have undertaken the theoretical and practical work that this book has introduced you to. It gives your clients confidence and it improves the quality of the healing they receive because they see that it is real, based on true understanding and training.

The Four Gates *Medicine for the Soul* Diploma offers you this proof. It requires a little more work from you than simply reading this book but it is worth the extra effort and once you qualify we will also add your name to our list of healers and refer clients to you.

We will send you more information on how to proceed if you would like to pursue your shamanic qualification. Simply email us (ross@thefourgates.org) and we will write back by return. Our website is www.thefourgates.org.

But let's begin with the most obvious and fundamental question: What is shamanism…

One

Journeying into the Shaman's World

In this Chapter

An introduction to shamanism, the shaman's crisis of initiation, the shamanic journey, the upper, middle and lower worlds, omens and synchronicities.

Suggested Reading

Please note: There is no *compulsory* reading for any of your work with this book. There is however a *suggested* reading list at the start of each chapter which relates to the texts referred to and is of use if you wish to read around the subject and deepen your knowledge. For this chapter the suggested texts are *Black Elk Speaks* by John Niehardt, *The World is as You Dream It* by John Perkins and *Shamanism: Archaic Techniques of Ecstasy* by Mircea Eliade.

Equipment Required

Again, there is no need to purchase any special equipment to be a student of shamanism and indeed most shamanic healing tools tend to be found natural objects such as feathers and rocks. In practice however most shamanic healers these days prefer to work with a drum or drumming tape and a rattle so it will be helpful for you to own or borrow one of these or to make your own.

What is Shamanism?

The word 'shaman' originates with the Tungus people of Siberia and has a specific usage there. More generally however it has come to mean 'one who sees' or 'one who knows' and is now used generically for anyone who works in a shamanic way to provide healing, counselling or divination which is undertaken in partnership with spirit guides, allies and helpers.

This way of working is the oldest psycho-spiritual tradition known to humankind. Ritual artefacts discovered in the African Rift Valley have been found to date back 400,000 years and cave paintings depicting shamanic scenes of shapeshifting (where the shaman takes on animal powers or transforms into animal or plant forms), such as those at Lascaux and Tassili, though not as old as this, certainly date back thousands of years.

It is only recently in this long history that healers and therapists have begun to compartmentalise their spiritual approaches and healing methods into various camps and specialisms (such as aromatherapy, reiki, massage, crystal healing and so on) and the shaman would originally work with all of these and more (many still do) to provide the right medicine for his or her people.

Many of the things we now accept as the inventions or discoveries of modern science and psychology are also to be found in shamanism and its traditions from thousands of years ago. So for example, physics now tells us that we live in a 'quantum universe' where all things are part of and mirror the whole, where all is comprised of energy and where this energy can be made to change its shape and form (e.g. from a particle to a wave) depending on our interactions with it.

In fact shamans have been saying the same thing for thousands of years, although they have used different words of course. Black Elk, the Sioux medicine man written about by John Niehardt in his book *Black Elk Speaks* was quoted 200 years before quantum physics for example, remarking that 'we are all one' and that all things are part of the whole, the 'sacred hoop' of life.

As for changing the nature and form of energy through our interactions with it, the Shuar people of the Amazon have long had an expression that 'the world is as you dream it' which says much the same thing – i.e. that we create our own reality by virtue of the way we view the world.

Shapeshifting, as exemplified in age-old cave images, is recognition of the fact that human beings can – and do – merge with other energies and forms of consciousness.

The Crisis of Shamanism

How do people become shamans? It begins with a calling – not always in the sense of a spiritual vocation which implies a desire on the part of the shaman-elect to become a shaman like someone who wishes to become a priest might have, but a calling by the spirits who have recognised the natural gifts and skills of that person and have chosen him to become their partner in the work they will do together.

Often the call begins as a whisper – with an awareness on the part of the shaman-to-be that the world is not quite as he has been taught to view it, that there are signs, subtleties and shades of meaning out there, not black and white, scientific or mathematical certainties. He may have 'special knowledge' – the ability to see, hear and know things that others do not for example, a future-seeing awareness of things about to happen or an 'active imagination' that sees things (spirits) that others can't.

If the shaman ignores these signs and does not explore what they mean the whispers from spirit will often get louder until they become a roar. If he still ignores them, he is likely to enter what it known as an initiatory crisis. A mysterious illness (of a mental, emotional, physical or spiritual nature – or even all four at once) may suddenly afflict him for example, a disease for which there is no known cause and often no orthodox cure. Such is the story of Black Elk, who was close to death as a child and could not be saved by medical healing, only by the spirits themselves.

The classical literature also describes people being struck by lightning, near-fatally wounded by wild animals or hit by a mysterious shower of rocks that falls from the sky. These may be literal descriptions of physical events but they also have a symbolic or mythic quality (lightning = enlightenment; shower of rocks = falling beneath a heavy load). The event takes the shaman-elect out of ordinary reality as he is required to lay in the relative isolation of a hospital bed or a healing room to recover from his injuries, or to enter the landscape of his mind and personal myths in the case of mental or emotional distress. He begins in this way to see beneath the veneer of the 'normal' world and more deeply into himself and the nature of reality.

What saves the shaman-to-be in all of these cases is the spirits. It is they who intervene, bringing him out of decline by magical means against the odds and often in impossible circumstances. This is the roar of the spirits – their proof and evidence for the shaman that there is more to the world than consensus reality and that by working with them he will be healthy and empowered.

Because the shaman has survived his encounter with illness he is not only stronger but knows the 'theory of disease' (in the words of Mircea Eliade) and can cure illness in others since he has first-hand experience of it. It is for this reason that shamans are called 'wounded healers' – they are not just dealing in concepts but in real experience because they have been hurt or ill themselves. Through this they learn about disease and how to negotiate with its spirit to make others well.

If in your life you have ever sensed a different order of reality, heard whispers from the Otherworld, seen things that others couldn't or had a sixth sense about things that people around you might have thought strange, unusual or uncommon, it is probably an indicator that the spirits have a calling for you too. Listen to it, explore it and find out more so the whisper does not become a roar. This is good advice too for clients who are struggling with emotional or even physical problems: that their circumstances could be a message that they should listen to because it may be a call for them to open up to the spiritual world and find their healing in that way.

The Shamanic Journey

Whatever else the shaman may be a specialist in (plant medicine, for example, or healing rituals) the key approach of all shamans, ancient and modern and across all cultures, is the shamanic journey: entering into a special state of consciousness that enables him or her to commune with the energy (or spirit) of the universe.

The Sora Indians believe for example that the shaman can command his soul to leave his body so the spirits may speak through him. In Siberia the shaman takes flight to the Otherworld to rescue lost souls. In Haiti the shaman (the Houngan or Mambo) is taught how to despatch his soul to Gine (a mythical location like Eden, thought to be the embodiment of primal Africa) so that Lwa (heavenly spirits) can take over his body and transmit their healing through him.

The journey then is a method for out-of-body travel by which the shaman may explore the spiritual universe, make contact with tutelary spirits, recover energy that has been lost or find out more about his client and her spiritual purpose.

In a modern context, the method below is the way to take a shamanic journey (for indigenous shamans the specific routes to trance will vary according to culture). Please don't try it yet though! That comes later. This is for the purposes of explanation only.

First, find a time and a place where you can be alone and undisturbed for 20 minutes or so, then dim the lights or cover your eyes and lie down on your back with your legs outstretched, and make yourself comfortable. This is the classical core shamanic posture for journeying, which also involves keeping your right arm by your side, fingers straight and the whole arm relaxed, then bending your left arm and placing it over your forehead so it shields your eyes. This is a trance posture that comes from the Amazonian Jivaro people according to Michael Harner and was described by him following field research there, in his book *The Way of the Shaman*. It may be worth adding that I have worked in the Amazon myself for more than a decade (although admittedly not among the Jivaro) and have *never* seen this posture used by indigenous people who, in the Amazon, use the visionary brew ayahuasca (see later chapters) to enter trance states during ceremonies where participants are expressly instructed to sit up instead of lying down and which often include a fair amount of bodily movement, not lying still. This posture has however become a staple practice in core shamanic circles and appears to produce results so I have no reason to question its effectiveness.

Most core shamanic journeys are taken to the sound of drumming, which encourages a specific state of trance and dream-like brain wave patterns to emerge, taking us into a deeper and more holistic experience of the world in its fullness. Again, among Amazonian tribes the drum is rarely if ever used for journeying (for one reason, a skin drum would last a very short time in the humidity of a rainforest). It is used more in Siberia, where Harner also conducted his research. Again, however, there is no doubting the effectiveness of the drum for inducing a trance state. You can drum for yourself (although you will not be able to maintain the posture of course), have a friend drum for you or use a drumming tape. All of these methods work.

Every journey is taken first and foremost to meet your spirit teachers and seek help or assistance with specific tasks or questions. Whatever the nature of your work in the Otherworld, even if you are journeying on behalf of another, you must always make contact with your own spirits first so they can help and protect you on your way. The only exception to this ever in fact is in this first chapter where you will be making exploratory journeys and finding your spirit guides. Again, do not do this yet though; just read the description of how to journey. There is a section later where you will practice the technique.

Expressing your intention – the purpose for your journey – and keeping this in mind is equally important as you journey. Intention is the energy that guides us and ensures we do not wander aimlessly in the Otherworlds. So the next thing is to express your intention by putting whatever question or purpose you have into a positive statement of intent. (Your first intent, normally, will be to meet your spirit guides and once this is done to ask whatever questions you have). So for example, the question 'Should I move home and live in another part of the country?' could be expressed positively and definitely as: 'My intention for this journey is to explore the outcome of moving to [whichever county or state appeals to you]'. This statement alerts the spirits to your purpose so they can work with you more effectively. To put this in a more shamanic way, it begins to direct your energy and the energies of the universe towards a specific focus. It also ensures that you do not get distracted because you have a clear and definite purpose in mind.

As soon as the drumming begins imagine yourself entering a place which will take you down into the Earth, such as a well or a cave (for a lower world journey – more on this later) or up into the sky via the branches of a tree or by climbing a ladder (if you are making an upper world journey). If your intention is a middle world journey – as it might be for example if you are working as psychopomp (more on this in a later chapter) – then imagine yourself disappearing into a strange mist or sailing away on a crystal ship to the 'Islands of the West' as Celtic shamans and the heroes of myth do in their legendary stories (all myths and legends contain at least a hint of shamanic technique and wisdom). Continue in your imagination until you reach your destination – the light of the Otherworld and the spirit beings who will be waiting there to help with your question – then let the journey unfold as it will so you no longer try to control it. Remember your intention throughout and if you lose your bearings at any time focus on the sound of the drum and come back to your purpose again.

Once you are in the Otherworld do not try to dictate the action that takes place or the information you receive. Just relax. Imagination is the bridge we use to cross to the Otherworld but once we are there the spirits are our guides. All we need do is receive.

Drumming tapes have a special call-back signal at the end to bring you back to ordinary reality and normal consciousness. When you hear this or when you are ready, retrace your steps out of the Otherworld and come back to normal awareness. Then write down your thoughts and feelings as well as the answers to your questions so you have a record you can refer back to.

The Shaman's Universe: The Three Cosmic Worlds

The Otherworld that the shaman journeys to is in fact divided into three realms which are known in modern Western shamanism as the upper, middle and lower worlds. Each has a different type of energy and feel to it and is occupied by different spirits with their own personalities.

Upper world. The upper world is an ethereal place populated by angel-like entities, wise beings and sages who normally take human (or human-like) forms. It often has a 'garden' feel or appearance and is experienced as light and airy and the spirits as welcoming, wry and humorous, like old friends. As with every-thing in shamanism (and in life) there are no fixed and absolute rules to this however so your experience may be different and equally valid but very often the landscape and spirits of the upper world do appear as they are described here, according to the reports of the shamans who journey there.

To enter the upper world you must of course go up (perhaps by visualising yourself climbing a tall tree). There must also be a sense that you are passing through a membrane of some kind. So that for example, having made your ascent, the sky that you reach will feel as if it has a slight resistance to it, as if it is a film of some kind that must be broken through. Making your way through this membrane is how you know for certain that you have entered the upper world. Without this sensation of passing through something you might not have reached the upper world at all.

Lower world. The lower world is the place of more primal and 'earthy' forces. In Haiti it is where the ancestors live and is sometimes known as 'the abysmal [as in deep] waters' but in most shamanic practices it has more of a jungle feel to it and is also the place of power animals – spirit entities that are more likely to appear in animal rather than human form, including fantastical or mythological beasts as well as those which can be found on Earth, even if in distant locations.

The lower world has less of a 'garden' and more of a primal sense to it. That is, it is less structured and 'manicured' and more natural and powerful. It is usually the place the shaman will go in order to retrieve power or seek guidance from ancestral spirits.

To enter the lower world you must visualise yourself making a descent into the earth through some natural opening (perhaps one that you know in ordinary reality) such as a cave, a well or the roots of a tree. The cave may slope downwards into darkness but it is a darkness in which you can still see clearly. It may have interesting features and passageways you can explore to see where each one leads and what other information may be found there. At some point during your explorations however you will notice a light which will be coming from the cave exit and is the light of the lower world. The shaman will make his way towards this and step through into another land, keeping his journeying intention in mind.

Middle world. The middle world is the energetic parallel of the everyday reality we are used to (everyday reality was described by Castaneda's shamanic mentor, don Juan, as 'the hard world of solid objects' and it is known in Haiti as 'the marketplace' because everything here is for sale in one way or another). Despite its appearance as made of solid and material things 'physical' reality is actually far from it. Modern science tells us that at the most fundamental level of existence all things are energy. In fact, I once shared a conference platform with quantum physicist and hyperspace theorist Michio Kaku (see for example his book *Hyperspace: A Scientific Odyssey Through Parallel Universes, Time Warps, and the 10th Dimension*, Anchor 1995) who commented that if you were able to compress all the truly solid bits of your body into one space and remove the energetic 'gaps' between them your physical body would actually be the size of your thumb. It is this energy that scientists and shamans both work with.

The middle world is also the realm of the ideas and thought-forms that go into the creation of the physical world since all things begin with an idea 'plucked from the ether' or 'received from a muse' before they are brought into being. Nothing – no great building or work of art or television programme or child – ever just happened; somebody had to dream it first, taking their inspiration from the intangible world of 'the invisibles' (or spirit).

Because the middle world is the parallel to our own it can sometimes be a challenging place to visit since it is occupied by beings like us and the entire mix of human nature (good and bad) is represented there. It is also the world that souls first visit after a person dies and if these deaths were sudden or unexpected there can be confusion, sorrow or anger among the spirits who dwell there, some of whom can also become lost or trapped. The middle world is the place the shaman must visit when undertaking soul retrieval or psychopomp work (more on these in later chapters) and he must therefore ensure that he is protected and filled with power before he visits this realm.

To reach the middle world imagine yourself entering a mytho-logical dimension, a place not unlike the world we are used to but with more of a fairytale feel to it – the other side of a strange mist, a deep forest or a place beneath the surface of still waters perhaps. Entering this mist or forest is passing through the veil. On the other side is the world you are seeking.

The mood of this place is often very different from the upper or lower worlds. Some describe it as 'grey', 'gloomy', 'eerie' or in some way 'sticky' where movement may be tiring or difficult. It is not always conceived like this of course but these are some of the terms I have heard students use. Perhaps the overriding sense is one of melancholy and the feeling that there are things present which cannot be seen – slightly unnerving.

Journeying Practice

The work of the shaman is practical and learned by experience. Now you understand the theory of journeying and the worlds of the shaman it is time to explore them. Your intention on these journeys is simply to practice your skills by visiting the Otherworlds, not to make contact with any of the beings or energies you might meet there. If you should happen to come into contact with other energies and they seem keen, excited or interested to speak with you (and they may do as our spirit allies are often delighted to see us when we first enter their worlds) be courteous and polite but firm and explain that you cannot speak with them on this occasion but you will return later to make contact between you.

For each journey:

- Prepare your space (by purifying and protecting it with incense and prayer etc)
- Assemble your equipment (your drum or drumming tape and anything else you may need)
- And be clear on your intention

In this case your intention might be a form of words along the lines of: 'My intention is to journey to the [upper, middle or lower] world to explore the terrain and familiarise myself with it' but find your own words if you can. The equipment needed is a drum or drumming tape.

Lower World Journey

Relax, lie down, close your eyes and begin drumming or start your tape. Express your intention a few times (out loud if you wish) to ensure you have it clear and fixed in your mind. Then follow this process:

- In your imagination see yourself standing in a clearing before a place (perhaps one you know) that in some way takes you down into the Earth (a cave, a well, the burrow of an animal etc). For the purpose of this journey I will use the example of a cave
- Enter the cave and begin to walk through it, exploring as you go. There may be more to see than first meets the eye
- You will be drawn to a light source which reveals the exit from the cave. Step through this threshold into the lower world
- Look around, explore. What does it look like to you? How does it feel? What is its mood? Do you see any objects, artefacts, pathways or other entities in this place? What else is around? Take your time and stay as long as you wish, making a mental note of areas you can explore on later journeys as you go deeper and further into the lower world
- When you are ready to leave or your drumming tape calls you back turn around and retrace your steps exactly, back to the cave entrance, through the tunnel and exit into the clearing you first had in mind before you went into the cave

- Begin to be aware of your body and your place in physical reality. Move your fingers and toes, feel the floor beneath you and gently open your eyes
- Make a note before you forget of all the things you have seen and experienced
- Sprinkle a little cold water on your face and take a drink. This will help ground you and bring you back to everyday consciousness

Leave a day or two before you begin your next journey to allow your realisations to sink in and your energies to settle. Be aware of your dreams and reveries and the other messages from your soul during this time as the information you have received may still be bubbling away in the mythical landscapes of your unconscious and other realisations may surface.

Upper World Journey

Relax, lie down, close your eyes and begin your drumming tape. Express your intention and ensure you have it clear and fixed in your mind then, as before, follow this process.

- See yourself standing in a clearing before a place that in some way takes you up into the sky. For the purpose of this journey I will use the example of the world tree – the axis mundi or mythical 'central post' of the Earth that connects all three worlds in the shamanic imagination (see the Clarification section which follows)
- Begin to climb the branches of this tree until you touch the sky and feel that there is a membrane of sorts that you are pushing against. Push through it into the upper world
- Look around, explore. What does it look like? How does it feel? What is its mood? Do you see any objects, artefacts, pathways or entities in this place? Make a mental note of what you see so you can explore it on later journeys

- When you are ready to leave or your drumming tape calls you back turn around and retrace your steps exactly, back through the membrane between worlds, down the branches of the world tree to the clearing you first had in mind
- Begin to be aware of your body and physical reality. Move your fingers and toes, feel the floor beneath you and gently open your eyes
- Make a note of all the things you have seen and experienced then sprinkle a little cold water on your face and take a drink

Once again, leave a day or two before you begin your next journey to allow your realisations to sink in and your energies to settle, and be aware of your dreams and reveries. Add these to your notes.

Middle World Journey

Because of the way the middle world is sometimes felt and perceived it is a good idea to protect yourself energetically before journeying there. Imagine a shield of light around you that crackles with energy and will not let anything through that you do not explicitly will in or allow. This energy-sphere infuses your body and reaches out and beyond your physical self to an arms length around you, making you totally impenetrable and full of power. When you feel brimming with power lie down and relax as before, close your eyes and begin your drumming tape. Express your intention a few times (out loud if you wish) so you have it clear in your mind.

- See yourself standing in a clearing as before in which there is the presence or possibility of a mythical divide between ordinary and non-ordinary reality. In Celtic myth this was sometimes perceived as passing behind a tree or into a forest or magical mist that could transport the shaman to the faery kingdom or Otherworld. Mist is the example I will use here

- See and feel yourself entering this mist and emerging in a different landscape which may be visibly similar to the one you just left but has a different quality or mood to it. This is the middle world. The transition is almost instant
- Look around, explore. What does it look like? How does it feel? What is its mood? Do you see objects, artefacts, pathways or entities in this place? Take your time and make a mental note of areas you can explore on later journeys
- When you are ready to leave or your drumming tape calls you back turn around and retrace your steps exactly, back through the mist which divides the worlds and to the clearing you first had in mind
- Begin to be aware of your body and your place in physical reality. Move your fingers and toes, feel the floor beneath you and gently open your eyes
- Make your notes then sprinkle a little cold water on your face and take a drink to ground yourself and bring you back to normal consciousness
- Once again, leave a few days between journeys to allow your realisations to sink in and your energies to settle and be aware of your dreams and reveries

Now you have experienced these Otherworlds and know the technique of journeying begin to practice on your own. Journey back to these places a few times and explore further so you can build a map of the worlds and know where places of power and healing may be found.

Clarification: The World Tree

Shamans conceive of a tree that stands at the very centre of the world and is a gateway to all the dimensions – seen and unseen – around us. It is the central point of balance that holds our world together. In the imagination this tree can be scaled for access to the upper world or its roots can be used as a ladder to the lower world. In some of the Celtic tales, by simply passing behind a tree (or entering a forest) a person could be taken into the world of 'faery' – the middle world.

In some cultures this tree symbolism is taken very literally. In Siberia, for example, one of the initiatory tests of the shaman-to-be is to scale a real tree while in a state of trance and carve a number of notches in the uppermost boughs, signifying his mastery of trance and shamanic journeying and his communion with spirit.

The world tree can be used as a gateway to all of the shamanic worlds and as a starting and exit point for any journey you take.

Omens and Synchronicities

I suggested that you pay attention to your dreams (keeping a dream journal is useful for this and will get you into the discipline of recording your dreams as soon as you wake) and also listen to the other messages from your soul between the journeys you take. This is because shamans believe that all things are alive and sources of information from the spirits who work with us. Dreams are the voice of the spirit world speaking through our souls.

Since all things are alive and have spirit there are other ways of receiving these messages too. Looking for omens, signs and synchronicities in everyday affairs and especially in nature is one example. For the Celts nature was 'the visible face of spirit' and what we see there has guidance for us.

Intention, as in all things shamanic, is paramount. If you set a question for the universe each day and make it your intention that your question *will* be answered then the things that happen to you, the people you bump into by 'accident' or events which occur seemingly at random – the shape of a cloud, an odd word overheard, a delay on the train that makes you late for a meeting – miraculously transform themselves and now contain information for you in answer to your question. In this way nature connects with the mythical landscapes of your soul. As the modern shamanic explorer Terence McKenna wrote, 'Nature is alive and talking to us. This is *not* a metaphor.'

Doing exactly this – setting a daily question and intention – is good practice for the shaman so begin it now. Not only will it enable you to deepen your connection with spirit and receive wider guidance from the world but these synchronicities can be important in your healing work (which we will look at in the next few chapters). Very often during healings for example you may catch sight of something 'out of the corner of your eye' – perhaps an everyday object in your home (a flower or a book for example) that suddenly has greater significance in the context of that healing. This is a message from spirit that there may be an answer for your client's well-being in that book or that the flower itself is important and connects to some event in her life. If you are alert and see the omen you will be able to incorporate it into your work; if you are not you may miss the most important thing in the healing, the very thing in fact that your client was drawn to you to hear.

Begin your practice of daily question and intention. Set the question each morning, remain vigilant for signs and omens during the day and then in the evening write down your thoughts and recollections. What is the central 'theme of the day' that emerges and how does this relate to the question you set? Is there an answer you can see or relate to in some way?

That is how we work with omens shamanically – by allowing the universe to speak with us in symbols, feelings and moods. Keep this practice up for at least a month because in coming chapters we will be moving on to healing and a deeper connection to spirit will stand you in good stead.

Quick Test 1

(Quick tests like this feature in every chapter as revision aids on the material you've covered so far. Pause and reflect on them but you don't need to write anything down even if you're following the Diploma route. The answers follow at the end of this book).

1. How might you define the word 'shaman' to someone who had no knowledge of shamanic practice?
2. Mircea Eliade in *Shamanism: Archaic Techniques of Ecstasy* described the shaman as a 'specialist in spirit' and a 'walker between worlds'. The shaman works in both worlds – those of spirit and everyday reality – and may be skilled in a number of healing practices that all have a spiritual aspect to them. Originally, therefore, the shaman made no distinction between any healing practices which brought relief to the client. With this in mind suggest three healing approaches that might be used in shamanism.
3. Eliade also described the shamanic journey as a form of ecstatic trance. But what exactly is a shamanic journey and why might it be undertaken?
4. List three things you should do in order to prepare for such a journey.
5. What are the two most important things to do in any shamanic journey?
6. List three characteristics (or things to look for) when journeying in the upper, middle and lower world.

Exercises

Practice your journeying, your dream journal work and your work with omens. Before you read the next chapter please also undertake these pieces of work which have a bearing on the subjects we will shortly look at. (If you intend to follow the Four Gates Diploma route please write down the work that you do in these Exercise sections so they can be sent to us later for feedback. Your report for each exercise should be 300-500 words in a Word format which can be sent as an email attachment).

Exercise 1: Journeying into the Day

Cast your mind back to a significant event or incident during the day – a meeting with someone for example – that seems in some way important to you. This is an event you will journey to. As well as allowing you to practice your journeying skills it also offers you a means of validation for this work because whatever the spirits tell you can be checked by asking the person concerned.

Let's say you met a friend for lunch and had a nice chat but as you walked away you had a sense that something might be troubling her, something that was never mentioned or spoken aloud. What gives you this sense?

Then make a journey to explore what was *not* said. The next time you meet your friend you can then ask, subtly, if something was (or is) wrong for her and if it was or is this... [whatever you have seen or sensed in your journey]. You are then in a position to offer help if you wish.

Diploma students: In your report, be clear on the following:

- The omen that alerted you to journey to this event
- The intention for your journey (what were the words you used?)
- Given this intention and the nature of your question did you think it best to take an upper, middle or lower world journey? Why?
- Describe your journey and what you discovered
- What feedback did you receive from your friend?

Exercise 2: Spiritual Hide and Seek

This is an exercise to be undertaken with a friend. It is like the childhood game of the same name, but here neither of you physically moves. Instead, ask your friend to hide in their imagination, choosing anywhere they wish. It might be a place they have actually visited and know from real life, somewhere they've seen on TV or a fantasyland from a story they have read. Ask them to take themselves to this place in their mind's eye but not to tell you where it is, only that they are hidden there and to have a good, clear picture of it.

Your intention is to track them by journeying to where they are hiding, using your skills of imagination to follow them. This might sound impossible – but you may also be surprised at how easily you find them and at what your imagination can do.

When you are sure you have found them in your journey retrace your steps and bring yourself back to normal consciousness. Tell your friend where she was hiding and listen to her feedback to see how accurate you were.

This is a skill that develops with practice so don't worry about 100% success the first few times (though you may be more accurate than you can believe right now). It is also one of the skills most important to the shaman as soul retrieval relies for example on finding lost soul parts that may also be hiding, confused or afraid in the Otherworlds. Take this journey a few times therefore and, if you can, with a number of different friends before you move on to the next chapter. Record your thoughts each time so you also build up a picture of the sort of people you find it most easy to trace. This may become significant in future when different sorts of clients ask for your help.

Two

Finding Your Power

In this Chapter

The true nature of power, life scripts and how we can give power away, exploring your own life script: the geis, Petty Tyrants, retrieving power/understanding the energy body, power animals, tutelary spirits, nature allies.

Reading for this Chapter

Since this chapter concerns power and for most people this will include notions of love and acceptance it is suggested that you also read and work through *Love's Simple Truths: Meditations on Rumi and The Path of The Heart* (Ross Heaven) which is available at Amazon Books and/or *The Way of The Lover: Rumi and the Spiritual Art of Love* (Ross Heaven). Others referred to in this chapter include *The Teachings of Don Juan* (Carlos Castaneda), *Shamanism* (Mircea Eliade) and *Of Water and the Spirit* (Malidoma Some).

Equipment Required

Drum or drumming tape
Rattle

A Note on this Chapter

Working with power can be difficult because it asks shamans and their clients to look at issues (for example of love and abandonment) in their own lives. It is important as apprentice healers that we do this, however, because it enables us to understand ourselves better and to purify ourselves so we meet our clients (and other people in our lives) from a place of wisdom and peace. It also means that we understand our clients better since they will in one way or another be struggling with the same issues as us. However, please proceed slowly and take a break from the work of this chapter whenever you need to. There is no rush and it is better to process and integrate what you learn than to speed through some of the exercises this section contains.

What Power Means

Most people in the Western world have an inauthentic relationship to what they take to be power. They do not know what real power is because they have never been taught to recognise it. For them, power is defined as Cadillacs and country homes, dotcom salaries and Gucci suits. But actually there are huge paradoxes in our beliefs about power, the first of which is that our most 'successful' people actually have little of it. Every businessman and woman who has 'made it' for example knows they must give up their lives to their business, working long hours away from their family, interests and passions – away from their humanity in fact – until they become part of the business itself, just as an engine is part of a car. The further up the corporate ladder they climb the less of a life they have. Andrew Carnegie, one of the richest people on Earth, was once asked why he continued to work when he had enough money to retire many times over. 'I've forgotten how to do anything else,' he said.

Those who 'make it' may have wealth, status, even 'celebrity' but they often have less freedom and genuine power than when they began and even that may have to be given away to 'subordinates' and intermediaries who shield them from reality. Those we most aspire to be – rock stars, movie gods or sports heroes for example – have people to look after them day and night. Agents, managers, PR people, secretaries, accountants, lawyers, bodyguards; these are the people who run the lives of the rich and famous and turn them into 'what the public wants'. 'Everything [is] designed to stop you growing up,' said Dougie

Payne, bass player with the rock band Travis. 'There are people running around doing everything for you so you don't mature as people until something serious happens, then you go whao, this is real life.'

Our dream of power is just that – a dream we live through force of habit and, as the philosopher Thomas Paine wrote, 'A long habit of not thinking a thing wrong gives it a superficial appearance of being right.' Waking up to this and stepping outside of society's 'power-programme' and habits in order to find real purpose is one of the most important things a shaman can therefore do. It allows him to reclaim his awareness of who he truly is and what it means for him and his client to be a 'true human' in the words of don Miguel, one of the shamans I work with in Peru.

Following the call of spirit, the shaman's initiatory crisis (see chapter one) will often show him through spiritual means that the dream of life he has been living is not all there is. Rather, he may have given his power away to what Celtic shamans call a geis, a scripted life.

The Geis: How we Live our Scripts

For the Celts, a geis (pronounced 'gesh') was a curse, taboo or sacred challenge made against a warrior, compelling him to do certain things or avoid other things, people or situations he might otherwise have been inclined to seek out and enjoy. The Hero's Quest – and the twists and turns of our mythological tales – arises from the warrior's struggle to avoid breaking his geis or alternatively to find a way around it. Usually the geis/curse was made against him by a parent, lover or other significant person in his life (the people from whom we learn our social roles and relationships to power) and the consequences of breaking it were severe.

The warrior Lleu was placed under geis by his mother Arianrhod, for example, that he would never have a name, bear arms or take a wife – the three initiatory rights traditionally conferred on a son when he attained manhood. Lleu's life story – his Heroic Quest – therefore became one of finding a wife and reclaiming his power. He overcame the first two curses by magical means and almost succeeded in finding a wife too (by creating, again through magic, the beautiful Blodeuwedd: the wife of flowers). She was unfaithful to him, however, so Lleu was never able to fully break his geis, the life story his mother had handed him.

Stories like these are not just idle tales; they contain shamanic psychology and principles of power. In modern terms for example Lleu's is a story of an overbearing mother intent on keeping her son a child because of her own needs, and of his attempts to free himself from control. It demonstrates one way (perhaps the first and most essential way) that power can be lost.

Exploring Your Own Life Script

This is an exercise to help you examine your own relationship to power.

Prepare your space as for any shamanic journey (see chapter one). Lie down, relax and breathe deeply. Now find an intention for this journey: to explore the patterns of your life and the way you are using power. Begin your drumming tape.

Stage 1: The Child's Vision

See yourself walking into a deep cave which descends into the Earth. Ahead of you, you see daylight where the tunnel ends. Beyond it is an open field. Walk towards the light and step out onto the grass. Look around, take your time.

You begin to sense that you are not alone here and your eye is drawn to a small figure on the horizon. You walk in that direction and as you get closer notice that the figure is that of a child who is sitting on the grass, hunched forward, gently crying.

As you draw closer and look into the face of this child you realise that it is yourself you are looking at; a younger you who is upset at something that is taking place in his or her life. Sit down and begin to comfort the child. He or she is delighted to see you and relaxed in your presence.

'What can I do to make things better?' you ask. 'If you had a single wish that could change things and make a better world for you what would it be? What would your vision of a perfect world look like?' The child thinks for a while and then answers. 'My perfect world would be one of...'

Come back to awareness and write down the child's answer. If you had to summarise this vision of a perfect world in just one word what would it be?

Write it down here:

_____

Stage 2: Saving the Child

Now close your eyes and relax into the journey again. Your intention is the same as before. Allow your consciousness to drift back to that field beyond the cave and to your younger self. Find yourself in conversation with this child once more. 'I understand your vision' you say. 'Now what can I do to make it real for you? What actions do I need to take to make this vision happen?' The child is silent for a moment and then answers you: 'These are the actions I'd like you to take to make this vision real...'

Acknowledge what he or she is telling you and remember it. If you are inspired to do so make the child a promise that you will take the actions needed to make this perfect world. Spend some time with the child now, then when you are ready to leave hug him or her to you and tell them you love them.

As you do so something remarkable happens. It is as if this boy or girl, now joyful and secure in your company, becomes a child of mist, of energy, pure spirit, and this mist is absorbed within you at your heart. You feel it entering you, filling you with power and childlike joy. And suddenly you two are one. This is a form of soul retrieval.

Turn and walk back across the field towards the cave, through the tunnel, back to your room, your body and to full consciousness, feeling invigorated, energised, awake and knowing that you now have another precious part of your soul.

Once again, write down the child's answer to your question: 'What actions do I need to take to make your vision real?' What are these actions needed to make a perfect world? If you had to summarise them as a single word what would it be?

Write it down here:

_____

Stage 3: What is Your Purpose in Life?

You should now have two words in front of you – one a 'vision' word and one an 'action' word. Now complete the sentence below by inserting these words in the appropriate places.

'My purpose is to create

_____

[vision word]

by acting with

_____

[action word] towards others.'

So, for example, your statement might be: 'My purpose is to create *happiness* by acting with *kindness* towards others.' By exploring your unconscious connections to your child-self at a time before your geis really took hold in your psyche what you now have is your purest mission in life; the thing you most need to know as a seeker of purpose and power – and the thing that your soul came here to do.

Stage 4: Your Shadow Self

There is more to this exercise, however, because if you rewrite your purpose to reflect its opposite (so, for example, in the case above, 'My purpose is to create *un*happiness by acting with *un*kindness towards others') you reveal your shadow-self which may be how you are using your energy in the pursuit of personal power during your more unconscious moments. Our shadow selves are the ones we have been taught by society to use most often when we go after power. They are revealed in our ambitions to get to the top, to win and to have authority over others in business, leadership or love during all of those times when we are not really thinking for ourselves.

Now that you see your shadow you can if you wish change it. What I'd like to propose is that you do two things:

- Firstly, reflect for a while on the times you have acted from your shadow in pursuit of power. Make an inventory so you are aware of the situations in which your shadow is more likely to emerge; in other words, those times when you did not create happiness because you acted unkindly or without full consciousness even though you may not have intended it. Be honest and fearless as you make this inventory, writing down all the times that you feel you failed in pursuit of your soul's higher purpose and intentions. It may upset you when you see this but knowledge of these things is also power so be courageous.
- Secondly, make a commitment to change: that whenever these situations arise in future again you will do something to break the pattern even if it is only walking away. Sometimes leaving the scene is a more genuine act of kindness, courage and power than staying with good intentions and letting our shadows take over.

Stage 5: Revealing the Geis

The positive mission statement you wrote is also your geis, looked at in a certain way. That is: we are often driven to change the things in our lives that cause us harm or discomfort. This is only natural, a basic survival instinct. But we are also prone to projection with rational minds that will try to protect us from harm – and from truth – at every turn. What you have written may be a projection itself. It is written in terms of making the world a better place but it is also an insight into your life and the things you need to change to make it better for yourself so you can stand in your own power.

Look again at the statement you wrote and ask yourself: 'Who did not act towards me in the way I have described?' So in the example above, who was it that did not make you happy or who acted unkindly and unconsciously towards you? Whoever they were or are they are likely to be people instrumental in your geis and one of the reasons you are seeking power and purpose in the way that you are. Spend a little time reflecting on this information then close your eyes, breathe into your heart and begin to journey. See yourself with this person who you have a connection to which is not serving you (or possibly them either) and which you recognise as draining your power in some way. See yourself sitting together in an empty room and within this room you also sit within a spiral of protective energy that separates you both.

Look at your bodies and you will notice that strands of energy connect you, from your body to his or hers. Notice where these strands connect. This will show you the relationship that existed between you. Is it a heart connection? Of the mind? Mainly physical? Also notice if there is a discrepancy in where these strands connect (e.g. do they leave your body at the heart but connect to his at the head?) This can suggest where miscommunication is taking place in your relationships or provide insight into where and how your power is taken by others.

When you are ready, say what needs to be said to the person

in front of you, speaking out loud, so you can forgive or make amends to them, accept their forgiveness, finish your business together, take back your power and say goodbye.

When the time is right you will see in your hand a knife you can use to cut the ties of energy between you. Breathe in as you do so to reclaim the power that was yours. This is a form of recapitulation. It does not hurt them or you; you are simply cutting through energy. As you free them and yourself from this connection that does not serve either of you watch them drift away, becoming more distant until they fade completely. Gently open your eyes and say 'I am free' – and be prepared to commit to that sentiment. Repeat this exercise whenever you need to and for every situation in which you feel your power was taken.

Really Letting Go

Strangely enough, the biggest problem for many people in using their power is often the fear of what might happen if they did. We are not used to power because we have the capacity for knowing and handling it trained out of us as we grow.

When our ties with the past are cut for example it may feel lonely, as if our old pain was actually a friend or a form of comfort to us and now we are alone and the future is uncertain. Before we began a series of power retrieval exercises on one workshop I asked the group to imagine the worst thing that could happen if they were fully in their power and could have anything they set their minds to. Two answers stand out, one from a female participant: 'I'd be happy' and one from a male: 'I'd get what I want'.

People have a hard time letting go of their suffering.
Out of a fear of the unknown they prefer suffering that is familiar
~ Thich Nhat Hanh

Loss of power is never entirely one-way since we must be in

agreement with those we allow to take power from us that we will accept their definitions of us and agree to the rewards we believe they offer us in return – acceptance, security, love, purpose, belonging, or whatever – even though the manifestation of these 'rewards' (status, fame, wealth etc) are themselves illusory, as we have seen.

Journey to explore the nature of power for yourself. Your intention is to answer these questions:

- What is the worst that could happen if I stood completely in my own power – and what will I do in response to this 'worst thing'?
- What rewards will I find from being in my power? How will it help me and how will I change?

Petty Tyrants

If we make the mistake of seeking purpose from others we feed those people our power and we feed from theirs, becoming characters in the drama of their lives as they are in ours. This can be serious when the person at the centre of that drama is a Petty Tyrant because there is no more ruthless thief of power. Paradoxically, however, a Petty Tyrant can also be one of our best allies for reclaiming power.

Petty Tyrants are those annoying, irritating, demanding and underhanded people who push our buttons, knock us off balance or make us lose our cool. They range in type and persona from bossy officials to aggressive bullies who present a threat to our safety. In all cases they leave us feeling disempowered, ungrounded, drawn into their drama and forced to see the world through their eyes because there is hardly ever room for negotiation or compromise with a tyrant. As an example, two of the Petty Tyrants we have all met are the Critic and the Victim.

Every bureaucrat, in their fixation on rules and procedures, has something of the Critic about them. In more mundane circumstances he or she is the nag for whom nothing you do is ever right or enough. Critics are slaves to their minds which are always looking for new faults to pick on. The ungrateful boss, partner or parent who is always on your case are examples of this sort of person. Their aim is to wear you down, chipping away at you for as long as you stay in their orbit until you eventually surrender and begin living by their rules.

You have two strategies for dealing with Critics. Because they are enslaved by their minds you can use the tools of the mind – reason and analysis – to take their arguments apart (emotional appeals rarely work). Assuming you are in the right, the Critic has little defence against a counter-argument that follows their own rules of logic and way of seeing the world. Your other option is simply to stand your ground and refuse to budge on anything that is said to you. The pure Critic, seeing that you are 'incapable of rational thought' will not waste energy on you for long.

The Victim is a different thing entirely. You might think it unfair to call someone who has been victimised a tyrant but that is often the power of the Victim for drawing you into their game. Victims can be expert dramatists who, without even appealing to you directly, can get you on their side and offering to sort out their problems – i.e. giving away your power – in minutes.

Victims appeal to your emotions and sense of pity. They look for rescuers because they have not dealt with their own issues of power or power-loss. In order to be 'saved' (fed with power) therefore they must attract both rescuers (attention) and perse-cutors (attention) so there is always a drama to be saved from and someone to save them from it. In this way they gain the attention they need and drain power from both sides at once.

Victims cannot allow themselves to actually be rescued; nor can they remain with one persecutor for long because once they are seen for what they are their methods become obvious – and Victims need to remain in the mystery in order to be empowered and then disempowered again.

Your best strategy with a Victim is to discuss their problems rationally and objectively with them, as well as their possible solutions and be prepared to leave it at that. If they truly want a resolution they then have the tools they need and can get on with it, taking the responsibility for their own lives which is otherwise lacking in their drama. The worst thing you can do is sort out their problems for them. They will not grow from this and you will end up labelled 'controlling'.

We can either treat Petty Tyrants like this as enemies to be resisted or avoided or as teachers to be learned from and, significantly, as mirrors to ourselves and sources of useful information since they reveal to us our real enemies: those within.

The tyrants we attract into our lives are there for a reason. We feel an affinity with them in some way and they stand as reflections of ourselves, so whoever it is that is upsetting you and in whatever way it is worth pausing to ask yourself what buttons they are actually pushing, which nerves they are getting on – and whether you recognise their behaviour in yourself.

The answer is probably yes. This is the gift of the tyrant: he or she allows us to discover new things about ourselves and the circumstances, situations or people we most often give our power away to. Indeed, so useful are Petty Tyrants in this respect that don Juan once advised Castaneda to actively go out and find one as he would make much more effective spiritual progress with input from a 'worthy opponent'.

Identifying Our Tyrants

We are most irritated by (and therefore give away power to) the people who remind us of the 'faults' or issues – the geis – we see in ourselves. Knowing this, we can use our tyrants to gain insight into ourselves and take back the power we have invested in these external people and things.

Close your eyes and breathe slowly and deeply. Begin a journey to a magical mirror which will show you the truth of yourself. In this mirror an image begins to appear of someone who annoys or irritates you, causes you some sort of conflict or pain in your life or pushes your buttons in some other way. It may not be the person you expected to see. Once this image is formed ask your reflection 'in what ways am I like you?' then listen to what it has to say.

Thank the person reflected there for the information they have given you and wish him or her well, then breathe out all those attributes you wish to rid yourself of, making a commitment to change. Open your eyes and make a note of what you have learned. These are the lessons you need to apply to your life in order to be powerful and free. You may find that it is easier said than done. Shamanism is not a fluffy new age practice where once you see a problem it is automatically solved. It won't be. It may take a lifetime's work. But at least you are aware of it now, a little more au fait with who 'you' are and you have begun your Hero's Quest; something which separates you from the majority.

Retrieving Your Power

We lose – or give away – our power in so many ways it is impossible to count them. They range from the trauma of dealing unskilfully with our Petty Tyrants (that is, giving in to their apparent power instead of using them as opportunities for growth) to the experience of lost love where we move into harmony with another and then watch that person leave, taking a part of us with them when they go.

Consider this though: Whatever happened has happened. It is gone. At a physical level you are somebody new. By the time you get to the end of this sentence 100,000 cells in your body will have died and been replaced. All the protein in your body is lost and renewed every 30 days. Multiply that by the number of days, weeks, months or years since the traumatic event and you can see that you *now* is not you *then*. You are wiser and more powerful. Whatever it was, you survived. And as the philosopher Nietzsche said: 'Whatever does not kill us makes us stronger.'

Knowing this on an intellectual level and feeling it in our spirits and guts are two different things, however, and often we need to make a gesture of power in order to feel whole again. This action is what shamans know as power retrieval.

Shamans believe that we don't just have a physical body but an energy body as well which takes the form of what Castaneda described as a 'luminous egg': a force field of power around us. Within this, in fact, we have four different types of body – the spiritual, emotional, mental and physical selves. Whenever we lose power, some of our energy is depleted so we do not function at our full capacity as human beings.

We may feel the effects of this across all our bodies. Spiritually we may experience 'loss of faith' that the spiritual world is there to help us. This may also manifest in a lack of hope that things will get better. Emotionally we may become depressed, listless, weepy or feel lost, alone, stuck or in some other way dis-spirited. Mentally we may feel anxious, stressed out, confused or unclear about where we are going or what to do next. Physically we may feel as if we have no energy or interest in life and may seek comfort in things we know to be unhealthy (smoking, drinking, drugs, addictive sex, a 'couch potato' lifestyle as we distract ourselves with TV, etc).

When the shaman recognises these signs in himself or another he is aware that loss of power is the cause for this 'dis-ease'. His solution is to retrieve power from the Otherworlds so that the energy body can be revitalised and energised in order to restore himself or his client to health. The classical method for doing so is power animal retrieval.

Power Animals

Power animals are spirit allies, typically to be found in the lower world. They are energies that take animal form. It is said that we all have a power animal that is always with us as a 'guardian spirit' whether we recognise this and develop our contact with it or not. When we decide to meet and work with our power animal this connection is strengthened and our ally can bring us greater energy and power.

There is an exchange or reciprocity in this. The animal ally offers you its strengths, abilities and qualities in return for something you offer it: the experience of being human by allowing its spiritual/energetic qualities into your body so they can work through you and the ally can see the world through your eyes.

Some shamans have many power animals as helpers (and so might you in time), each with a different purpose, personality and aspect of power. The animal itself will tell you its purpose but this can sometimes also be sensed by what the animal represents. For example a white horse might for you symbolise freedom; a hawk might represent the power to 'soar above' a problem but to swoop down at speed to pick off a particular issue when necessary; a bear might be a symbol of strength and vitality while a mouse suggests the ability to hide and get into the smallest gaps and most well-defended places to find food or a safe space... and so on.

Through observation and dialogue with the power animal/s you find you will learn which energies you most need in your life and how best to work with them so you have the power most useful to you.

Power Animal Retrieval

This is a lower world journey, to be taken in the way you are now familiar with (revise chapter one).

As soon as you enter the lower world look for running water – a stream or a river for example – and follow it back to its source, the place it first emerges from the Earth. Here you will find your power animal waiting for you.

Shamans believe that many animals – representing different

archetypal or spiritual energies – wish to work with us and it may be that you encounter a number on your journey so how will you know which animal is there for you now? Shamanic lore has it that this animal will reveal itself four times. Perhaps you see a particular animal on four occasions or perhaps only glimpse parts of it. Either is fine as long as it is seen in some way on four occasions during your single journey. When this is done simply ask the animal if it is the one you most need to work with at this time, how it will work with you and what it wants from you in return. Ask any other questions you also want answers to as well bearing in mind that this animal has always been with you and knows you and your life story (and geis) better than anyone.

If there are other animals that also want to work with you remember that you can return on future journeys so wish them well for now and promise to come back for them. It is not recommended that you retrieve more than one animal power at a time because, just like making a new friend, you need to spend some time with it in order to really know it and make it part of your world.

When your dialogue with your power animal is finished hug the animal to you (actually raise your arms in ordinary reality as well) and draw its energy into you. Feel its power and qualities enter your body as you now cross your hands over your heart. Then, returning to normal consciousness, take your rattle and shake it around your heart, torso and then your entire body to seal in this new energy.

Your power animal's energy then needs to be integrated into your body so begin to move like your animal would. If there is a sound it wants to make let this come out. Keep this up for a few minutes or until you feel a natural desire to stop. This is a signal that its energy has now joined with yours.

Shamans are known as 'walkers between worlds' (Eliade) – the spiritual and the material – and there are three ways for you to work with this power which cross all three of the worlds:

- In non-ordinary reality you can journey to this ally any time you need guidance, protection, answers or support.
- In ordinary reality assemble images or other representations of your power animal to strengthen your connection to its powers so they are more potently felt in your life.
- In non-ordinary/ordinary reality (a combination of the two states) merge with your power animal. This is a form of shapeshifting where you relax your hold just slightly over your sense of who you are and allow some of the energy of your power animal to come through you (a little like channelling). This fills you with power and is a device for self-protection and empowerment when you are facing difficult situations in everyday life or when you begin healing work with a client.

Practice all of these ways of working with your ally.

Tutelary Spirits

'Power animals', in shamanic understanding, are typically to be found in the lower world but we have allies in the upper world too. Here though they take the form of human-like entities or wise and angelic beings. Shamans say they are evolved souls who once were human and who have been given the choice to escape the wheel of death-and-rebirth because of the advanced work they have done on Earth. Instead of thinking only of their own freedom though they take pity on we 'poor, sick, suffering souls', aware that human life in this world of illusion and pain is the hardest journey of all. Their intention is to guide and help us.

These entities are not like animal spirits in the sense that their energies can be taken into and assimilated by us; rather, they are guides we can visit in our journeys to ask for advice and counsel or to see the truth of a particular situation. Theirs is a world of wisdom and information, which is not to say that they cannot also offer more practical support but usually their help takes the form of insights delivered as if by a caring parent who throws his arm around you and says 'Well, when I had the same problems as you this is what I did about it...'. Once again, knowledge is power.

To meet with your tutelary spirit take an upper world journey (see chapter one) with the intention of 'Meeting my ally and guide as a source of information and power'.

When you reach the upper world, begin to explore, spiralling out from your point of entry so that by retracing the spiral you can easily find your way back. Look for mountains, gardens that seem cared for, arbours, dwelling places and houses, and so on. This is how the upper world is most often perceived and it is in one of these places that your guide will be waiting for you.

Your meeting will tend to be civilised and light-hearted (one of my guides is a Chinese sage and his first action is always to make tea!) like meeting a friend or perhaps a relative you haven't seen for some time. Ask any questions you wish and begin to form your relationship. When you feel it is time to leave be guided by them as to how you cement your friendship. Some guides will hug you; some are more 'formal' and offer a handshake or a smile. Knowing that you can return here at any time, retrace your steps and exit the upper world.

Nature Allies

There are allies for us in the middle world too – the energetic parallel of our everyday reality. In Haiti this world is simply known as Nature, the purest expression of God's dreaming. To the Celts as well, nature was 'the visible face of spirit'.

Nature allies are especially important for healing work. When we deal in spirit extraction for example (discussed in a later chapter), we remove energies from a client that are not useful to him or her but we then need somewhere to put these energies.

Usually this is a place in nature, whether a tree, a hillside, a lake or a sea. We can also use these natural allies as a source of power for ourselves.

To work with these spirits choose a place in nature that you know and like in ordinary reality and which is not too distant from you (a country park, a hillside you sometimes walk on, etc) and journey shamanically to this place. Your intention is 'To meet with a nature spirit who will be my ally in healing and empowerment work'.

As you walk in the Otherworld be alert to the things that may call you – a tree, a boulder, a pool, etc – and allow yourself to be drawn to any one of these that signals most strongly to you. Sit down before it and let yourself blend with it so its essence begins to emerge. The African medicine man Malidoma Some writes in his book *Of Water and the Spirit* about his Otherworldly encounter with a spirit who emerged from a tree in the form of 'a beautiful green lady'. 'I wondered how I had never seen her before,' he said. Something similar may be the case for you.

Explain your purpose to this spirit and ask for its assistance in your search for power and healing. Notice how it responds and the form in which it offers you power (it is not unusual to be given a symbolic 'gift' of some kind). Also ask what you can do in return. And then come back to normal consciousness.

During the next few days make a visit in ordinary reality to this place that is now your ally and leave a gift there (whatever the spirit has asked for in return for helping you). Spend a little time there too, reinforcing your relationship and taking in the healing calm and power of this place.

Castaneda called such places 'places of power'. They are where the spirit is strongest and resonates most with your own. You will always find information and healing in such places and this is also a source of power.

Quick Test 2

1. Why might wealth and fame, etc – the things we in the West regard as symbols of power – actually be disempowering?
2. What do shamans mean when they talk of geis?
3. Why might forgiveness be a means of retrieving power for yourself?
4. What is a Petty Tyrant?

Exercises

Continue to practice your journeying, your dream journal work and journey again to your allies to deepen your connection. Before you read the next chapter please also do these pieces of work.

Exercise 1: How Power is Lost

Make a journey to your tutelary spirit (upper world) and ask to be shown the circumstances in your life when you have (or once had) a tendency to give away or lose power to others. What is the central theme that emerges from what you are shown? Write it down – in one word if you can. Then make a second journey and ask for a simple ritual you can perform to learn the lessons of – and then take back power from – this central theme.

Exercise 2: Maintaining Power

Make a journey to your power animal (lower world) and ask for a ritual of protection, a power song, a symbol or some other 'charm' or 'glamour' you can use to defend against your tendency to give away power in these situations. Perform the ritual if you are shown one or make the power object or charm or sing the song you are given.

Three

Tools and Techniques of Power

In this Chapter

Shamanic tools and techniques for raising, using and manipulating energy, including sacred sounds, the song of the shaman, smudge, crystal medicine, stones, plant spirit medicine, feathers, candles, prayer, eggs, walks of attention, gazing, sigils and symbols of power, trance postures.

Reading for this Chapter

None required. Books referred to include *Ecstatic Body Postures* (Belinda Gore) and *Where the Spirits Ride the Wind* (Felicitas D Goodman)

Equipment Required

Drum or drumming tape
Rattle
Other medicine tools referred to (optional)

Shamanic Power in the Form of Healing Tools

In the next chapters we look at the shamanic healing practices of soul retrieval, spirit extraction and energy balancing. All of these techniques often use specific shamanic tools. This chapter outlines the use of these tools and gives you an opportunity to familiarise yourself with them.

To be clear, however: when people talk of shamanic 'tools' there is often a tendency to imagine that it is the item itself that does the work or delivers the healing. In fact, for the shaman, *it is not the drum or the rattle that heals but the spirit it contains.* Shamans mean this literally and some do not work with tools at all, allowing the spirit to infuse them instead and working with their bare hands. This is so in the Philippines where bare-hand healers use psychic and spiritual powers to open up the body of a patient and remove by hand any physical problems or blockages they see. It is similar in Haiti where the shaman, deep in trance and possessed by angel-like spirits called Lwa may only need to touch someone to send a healing charge into them. I have experienced similar approaches in Cusco, Peru, as well, where the healer don Eduardo used reiki-like methods in a healing session, holding his hands over my body and using spiritual power to suck out bad energy and cast it away.

Shamanic tools are not essential for healing, then, but they *can* be used to empower the shaman and the client. There are many reasons for this according to the nature and purpose of the tool itself. Mostly they are used because they make it easier and clearer for the shaman to see where client energies are blocked, because they help the client in some specific way or because the shaman has a particular affinity with the spirit of that tool and works with the spirit itself to perform his healings.

Sacred Sounds

The shaman uses sound to shift his consciousness and that of his client and to open up the spiritual universe. Through the rhythmic beating of the drum and shaking of the rattle (his two primary tools) he is able to enter the state of trance necessary to become a 'hollow bone' for the spirits and get his ego and rational mind out of the way so it will not intrude upon and veto his insights and intuition.

Scientifically, it has been shown that drumming (or rattling) at a rate of around 220 beats a minute produces a shift in consciousness, taking brain waves into a deeper state most associated with dreaming and visionary experiences. It has also been found that drumming or being in the presence of a drum being played releases endorphins (the body's natural feel-good chemicals) into the bloodstream, producing feelings of well-being. This is healing in itself. While this is new to science however, shamans discovered these effects for themselves thousands of years ago.

For shamans the drum is also a portal which can be journeyed into and through in its own right, the shaman merging with its spirit and/or entering the Otherworlds through it. The spirit of the drum can then work through the shaman and carry out healings of its own. Sometimes this is all a client may need to feel better in him or herself.

In some cultures sacred sound extends to the use of gongs, bells, songs and singing bowls. In shamanic healings these have a particular use. When played over or next to the client's body they produce vibrational changes in the energy field, helping to release blockages and encourage energies to flow. Higher-pitched sounds such as bells are used in the Chinese practice of feng shui for example to disperse pools of stagnant energy that can gather in the corners of rooms. The effect is similar when used on the body.

Explorations

1. Practice with your drum until you can sustain a rhythm of 200-220 beats per minute and keep this up for ten minutes or so. Then bring the drum up closer to your shoulder and allow yourself to 'dream' into it and hear the voice of its spirit, letting the drum find its own rhythm so the spirit can speak. Hear what it has to tell you.

2. Practice seeing your drum as a doorway to the Otherworlds. As you play, journey into and through the drum itself and into the energetic or spiritual universe. Set your intent: 'To visit the upper, middle or lower world [choose one] through the portal of the drum'. You may find this faster and equally (or even more) effective than the classical routes of climbing a tree or entering the Earth

through a cave, etc.

3. The drum is composed of skin and wood. The wood represents the world tree – the symbolic tree that stands at the centre of the shamanic universe and links all three of the shaman's worlds. The skin represents animal powers and through these, stands for all animals. The drum is more than an object therefore; it is an agent of both the animal and plant kingdoms and contains wisdom and power because of this. Begin to access these powers by journeying to your drum and exploring the universe it contains. Develop a relationship with your drum as an ally for healing and empowerment by introducing yourself to it and explaining your healing intentions so the drum knows your purpose and can help you. On your journey also ask two specific things: *What is the name of your drum* and *how does it want to be fed*? All spirits need to be fed so they are energised and can do their work. A drum may ask for sage smoke to be blown over it for example – see below – or perhaps rose water to be rubbed into it. These and similar things are typical foods of the drum.

The song of the shaman

Chants, mantras and sacred songs are other tools of the shaman where he allows the spirits to sing through him, bringing healing words and tunes to empower and soothe the soul or bring it home from where it is lost.

In the Amazon ayahuasca shamans sing icaros during their ceremonies. These are songs taught to them by the plants of the rainforest and talk of the power of nature to cleanse and heal. As the shaman sings he guides participants in the ceremony to places of healing in the Otherworlds where the spirits will greet them and provide whatever insights or healing they may need to feel well and whole again (more on this in a later chapter). Sound is a form of vibrational medicine. The expert shaman is also able to use his song precisely, like a surgeon's knife, to create physical changes.

In 'core' shamanism there is the concept of the Power Song: a magical tune, sometimes with clear and understandable words, sometimes in meta-language that is given to a shaman by his power animals or allies. He can sing this for himself to fill his body with power (before a healing for example) or sing it into the energy body of a client so it can heal her.

Exploration

Journey to your power animal/s and ask to be given a song of power that you can use for a similar purpose. As the song is given to you sing it out loud and, if you can, record it on a tape machine which runs throughout your journey. This will make it easier to remember.

Returning to normal consciousness, write down the song in your journal. If the words are not in a clear and understandable language write them down phonetically and then 'dream' into the page to find a translation that becomes intuitively clear to you. Write this alongside the words as they were given and then memorise your song.

Smudge

Smudge sticks are bundles of herbs (often based around sage) which are set alight and the smoke used to cleanse and purify the client, the shaman and the tools he will use before a ritual or healing takes place. Sage smoke is traditional among Native American shamans for carrying prayers to the spirits for healings or blessings.

When used in cleansings, smudge can act as a useful diagnostic tool as well. The smoke should naturally 'stick' to a client (or yourself). If, however, the smoke appears to be pushed away from the body or alternatively is 'sucked in' at certain points this can be an indication that power has been lost from that part of the energy body or that a spirit intrusion is present which needs to be removed (see next chapters).

Exploration

Practice using smudge on yourself or friends. One technique is to circle the smudge stick three times around the crown of the head then bring it down the body to the heart and do the same. Your friend should stand with arms outstretched at the sides and you then trace the smoke along the underside of his or her arms and then over the tops. Then trace the smoke down the torso (with three clockwise circles over the solar plexus) and the legs. Ask your friend to raise their feet and draw the smoke under them too. Then do the same on the back of the body. Notice where the smoke goes as you do this. Are there any points of the body where the smoke seems to cling more than others or is pushed away? These may be areas for healing attention or where your friend is experiencing some physical pain.

Crystal Medicine

The science of crystals is now well-established and a great deal of information is available to explain which crystals to use in various circumstances, how they should be used and what ailments they cure. All of this is quite at odds, however, with the shaman's use and understanding of crystals.

Once again, the shaman is concerned with the spirit of the crystal he uses, not its physical properties. He has no interest per se in whether a crystal with six sides is better than one with four or whether clear quartz is more effective than rose quartz for drawing in love and opening the heart. His reason for using them is because the spirits have suggested their appropriateness for a particular client and have led him to a specific crystal he will use.

Crystals are most effective in channelling spiritual energies into a client when the shaman calls these with intent. So, for example, if a shaman recognises that a client is less powerful or has less energy than she could have he will journey to his allies to recover power for her and may then use a crystal to 'inject' this into her energy body, holding the crystal like a wand or a syringe or else laying them around his client's body and willing them to transmit power into her.

Crystals can also be used to map the energy body and begin to focus power into a client while the shaman works on other aspects of healing (there is more on this in an upcoming chapter). In either circumstance it is the shaman's relationship with the spirit of the crystal not his reliance on textbook guidance as to how these crystals 'should' be used that produces the healing effects.

Exploration

Make a visit in ordinary reality to a crystal shop and hold your hands over the crystals on display. You may feel a tingling sensation or a change in temperature if you are called by a particular crystal, the spirit of which wishes to work with you in your healings. If this is so you may, if you wish, answer this call by buying a few of these crystals and starting a collection of your own.

Then journey into your crystals in the same way you did with the drum in order to make a connection with them. Meet with the spirit of the crystal and ask how it can help you, how you will work together and how the crystal is to be 'fed'.

It is usual after a crystal has been used in a client healing to cleanse it so that energies from that client do not stick to the crystal and become transmitted to another client during a different healing. Typical ways of cleansing include washing in salt water, burying them in the earth for a few days or leaving them out under the sun and moon for a full day and night. The spirit of the crystal will have its own preference so make a second journey to the crystal and ask the spirit how it wishes to be cleansed. Follow this guidance after every healing you do.

Stones

Stones have a different energy to crystals. Naturally and without any request from the shaman they will remove negative energies and replace them with grounding and stabilising power.

They can be used in two main ways: either by finding a place in nature where you can simply sit with them, allowing yourself to relax into their energy field and speaking your problems out loud so you can be heard and comforted, or in a meditation where you lie quietly with the stones and let them soothe away your worries, as below.

Exploration

For this meditation you will need three (preferably flat, white, round) stones. Hold one in each hand and place the third on the point in your body where you feel you need healing.

- Crown: for spiritual problems or issues around connection and community
- Brow: to develop intuitive or psychic abilities
- Throat: for empowerment in matters of truth and your ability to speak it
- Heart: for emotional issues and to develop compassion
- Solar Plexus: to develop a stronger will and power of intent
- Base/Genitals: for greater security and sexual connection
- Soles of the Feet: for grounding and greater 'under standing'

Simply lie still, letting the stones do their work for fifteen minutes or so. (If you fall asleep, this is fine). Wash the stones in cold salt water (or, having journeyed to them, cleanse them in some other appropriate way). Use this meditation whenever you feel tired or need more spiritual energy.

Plant Spirit Medicine

Shamans are often expert herbalists but once again it is not the chemical properties of plants that interest them, it is their spiritual powers. Some plants, typically visionary in nature (such as ayahuasca, San Pedro, peyote, fly agaric and so on) are known as 'teacher plants' and open specific doorways into the Otherworlds but all plants are a means of communion with spirit.

In Haiti, the great healing spirit of Nature and the forests is Gran Bwa (the name means 'Big Wood') who is depicted as a combination of man and leaf, suggesting once again that all plants are alive and contain spirits which have an affinity and liking for human beings.

Plants may speak to the shaman during a journey and recommend themselves for his client. They can then be prepared as a medicine by the shaman and the mixture given to the client in the way recommended by the spirits. (There is more on plant spirit medicines in a later chapter).

Plants and their aromas also have magical uses to change a person's luck, give them energy or draw love and success, as is the case with these examples of oils from the New Orleans Hoodoo ('root doctor') tradition:

Vision Oil

To enhance psychic awareness, anoint the forehead with the following extracts or aromatherapy oils, held in a base oil of sunflower:

4 drops Lemongrass
2 drops Bay
1 drop Nutmeg

Peace Oil

Wear when nervous or upset to calm you down. Stand before a mirror and while looking into your eyes in the reflection, anoint your body with the following extracts or aromatherapy oils, held in a base oil of sunflower:

   3 drops Ylang-ylang
   3 drops Lavender
   2 drops Camomile
   1 drop Rose absolute

As you apply the oil say to yourself: 'I am strong, I am a child of God, and I can do anything for nothing is impossible to God!'

Energy Oil

Wear when feeling depleted, ill, or to strengthen energy reserves. Anoint your body with the following extracts or aromatherapy oils, held in a base oil of sunflower:

   4 drops Orange
   2 drops Lime
   1 drop Cardamom

Love and Attraction Oil

Prepare a perfumed oil using 2 ounces of almond oil as the base. Add 7 drops of rose water or 7 drops rose essential oil, 3 drops of lemon extract, juice or essential oil, one vanilla bean or 7 drops vanilla extract or essential oil. Add to the mixture a sprinkling of gold glitter or two gold stars. Anoint the pulse points before going out or add to bathwater for a love attraction bath.

Exploration

To get to know the spirit of a particular plant shamans often follow a very bland diet (based on plain rice and water) as they ingest the plants they are interested in. They may keep this diet up for a few days or a few weeks, taking the plant on a daily basis so it speaks its secrets to them and its spirit is merged with their own. If you (and your doctor) are happy that there are no contraindications try this diet yourself for a few days, eating only bland food that is not spiced in any way and does not contain salt, sugar, oils or lemon juice. Meat is to be avoided. Choose a plant (herb) that you wish to develop a relationship with and eat it or drink a tea made from it two times a day (morning and night) focussing on it and 'dreaming' yourself into its qualities during this time. After a few days make a note of all you have learned from the spirit of the plant and then compare this with the information you find in a herbal encyclopaedia. How does the spirit of the plant compare with the standard information you read there? Are there similarities or differences?

Feathers

In the shaman's hands feathers become surgical instruments and are often used in spirit extraction work. The blade of the feather, run over the energy body (a few inches above the physical body) will dip when an area of low energy is detected. The feather may also shake or move upwards when it detects intrusive energies of some kind. Seeing this, the shaman is able to use the tip of the feather like a knife to pick out the energies he wishes to remove.

Explorations

1. Shamanic healing is covered in a later chapter and you are not encouraged yet to experiment with healing using feathers. Do, however, begin to make a collection of feathers of your own by taking some walks in nature and allowing yourself to be drawn to any you find on your path. Take these home and smudge them (see above) in order to cleanse them and then journey in the normal way to the bird-spirit they contain. Explain your healing

purpose and be guided by what its spirit tells you about ways in which the feather might be used to heal.

2. Practice running the feather down your energy body and perhaps that of a friend. The more you use feathers the more sensitive you become to their energies. Move the feather very slowly over the body. A loose grip allows it to move freely when it senses a change in the energy system. Do not go any further with healing for now, simply get used to the technique of handling feathers in this way.

Candles

Candles are another means of spirit contact and are often used in conjunction with prayer (see below). In Haiti the spirits are fed by offering them a sacrifice, a word which means 'sacred offering', so the sacrifice itself is often just a plate of the same food as the person who makes the offering is eating but it is given in the spirit of love and gratitude. A candle is placed at the centre of the plate and the flame carries the energy of the food to the spirits.

There are hundreds of spirits in the Haitian tradition, all of whom can be appealed to for specific outcomes. The chart below gives five of the most popular and powerful of these spirits and lists the types of offerings that can be made to them. Each spirit also has a certain colour associated with it and this is reflected in the choice of candle.

Your Desire	Spirit	Characteristics	Candle Colour	Offering
Love	Erzuli	Female spirit, goddess of love in all its forms	Pink	Chocolates, perfume, white wine or champagne
Power				
New job, more pay, etc	Ogoun	Male warrior spirit often represented as a General, but also expresses power in diplomacy, negotiation skills, and so on	Red	Dark rum, cigars
Self-knowledge	La Siren	Female spirit of the oceans, the deep unconscious, and feminine principles	Light Blue	Melon, seashells, salt water
Blessings (especially for children) and sense of direction in life	Baron	Father of ancestral spirits and of children (death-rebirth); guardian of the crossroads and of choices about life paths	Purple	Hot red peppers, mixed spice, dark rum, cigars
Health and healing	Gran Bwa	Male spirit of nature and the power of plants to heal	Green	Soil, unsalted water, a tea light candle to represent the sun

Exploration

Choose one of the qualities above that you would like in your life and feed the appropriate spirit for seven days. Notice how your life may change as a consequence.

Prayer

Prayer is focussed intention, an act of will and a desire for a specific outcome that is released to the universe so the spirits may do their work for you. There has been some interesting research into the power of prayer and intention in healing physical disease. In one experiment patients who had just undergone heart surgery were prayed for without being told this was happening. A second group who also had surgery received no prayers, only standard medical care. The results showed that the first group healed much faster and better than the second. All other factors remained the same. The researchers had to conclude that prayer made a difference.

Every song of the shaman, every healing act he makes, is also a form of prayer. In Mongolia the prayerful calling for a blessing is known as an algysh. This is the algysh of a shaman asking for blessings for his children:

With golden hair, you are my children.
Let your mountain pass to cross over be low
Let your horses be fast
Let your food be satisfying.
You are beautiful, my children.
Let your river crossing be shallow
Let your path be fulfilled
Let your happiness be complete.
My abundant children
Let them sing their charming songs
Let them carry out their tasks
Let them have friends to be together with

Exploration

In the Western world we are often put off prayer because of the religious dogma associated with it. If we regard prayer as intention, however, we begin to see that it is important to be able to call to spirit and express our needs. Develop a relationship with prayer by creating your own algysh like the one above for something or someone who is dear to you.

Eggs

On the face of it this is a strange one and yet eggs are used widely in shamanism (everywhere from Peru to the European Romani tradition) to represent the human soul. They are used in diagnosis to reveal the state of the soul and to help with necessary healing.

Diagnostically the egg is gently rolled or stroked over the body and then broken into a glass of water, a process known as *limpia* in Peru. Careful attention is paid to how the egg white begins to move in the water. The yolk represents the physical body as well as the energy body or soul (the top of the yolk is the head; the bottom of the yolk the feet, facing forwards as you look at it).

The way the white clings to the yolk or moves away from it signals disturbances within the energy field that surrounds the body. A lump of white on the lower right for example might suggest a problem with the kidneys. A long strand of white drifting up from the top of the yolk however might suggest a strong connection to spirit and to the divine energies of the universe. A degree of intuition and almost journeying into the egg is required to read signs like this that it offers to the shaman.

Once the diagnosis is complete a second egg, still in its shell, is used to massage the area of the body where the disturbance is seen. The egg will absorb negativity and is then taken outside and buried in a place where it is unlikely to be dug up or disturbed by an animal or human being. (Also see the forthcoming chapter on spirit extraction medicine).

A slightly different approach is adopted in New Orleans tradition. Here the illness is drawn into one or more eggs in a similar way and these are then taken to a river. An offering is made to the water spirits so they will take away the illness now held by the eggs. They are then thrown into the river. You (or your client) must then walk quickly away, never looking back until you reach your home and seal the threshold of the doors and windows using salt (and lime or lemon juice if you wish) so the illness or problem the egg extraction has cured cannot find its way back to you again.

Exploration

Try egg diagnosis for yourself. Gently roll the egg downwards over your body and then break it into a glass of water and watch how the white begins to separate from the yolk. Note the areas of the body this corresponds to. Does this diagnosis seem relevant to you in any way – for example, have you experienced any pain or discomfort in the areas the egg white suggests?

Walks of Attention

Carlos Castaneda is credited with introducing the term 'walk of attention' but in fact moving meditations like this are known in all cultures and not only to the Toltecs of Mexico.

A walk of attention is a way for a shaman to be in his or her power by experiencing the energy body and using it to relate to the world around him. Most of us are in a hurry to get from A to B so we do not notice subtle changes in our energies or those of the world or how these two energy systems interrelate. During the walk of attention, however, walking becomes a deliberate act. The pace is slow and the shaman's attention is shared between ordinary and non-ordinary reality (he literally walks between worlds) as he focuses his awareness on his solar plexus, the place of his will, and allows his body to be led from this point. His eyes remain on the ground so he is somewhat inward-looking. In this way he can cover large distances without tiring because his power is conserved. At the same time his consciousness is shifted into a slightly altered state and he is able to touch his power.

Exploration

Find a place in nature where you are able to walk freely. Take your attention to your solar plexus. Walk deliberately, with your eyes down and your energy leading you from the stomach. See, if you can, tendrils of energy emerge from your solar area and wind themselves around objects in the environment as if you are being pulled effortlessly towards them by these energy fibres. Hold an intention in mind as well (perhaps to find feathers or stones that you can use in healing work) and allow the spirit of the landscape to lead you towards them. In this way you will be practising your dreaming skills as well as accessing your power.

Gazing

Gazing is another Castaneda term. It refers to the practice of seeing reality in a different way, almost the opposite of how it is normally presented to us or we have been taught to see it. So for example, in gazing we deliberately do *not* see the tree in front of us; instead we see a form made of composite shapes and shadows. Or we see a sky with a cut-out form in it (which convention would call a tree); we do not see the tree imposed on the sky.

Gazing is an important skill of the shaman since there will come a time in healing work when he must look at his client's body in this way, seeing not the physical self but the energy between the atoms which is the real stuff we are composed of. It is this energy that the shaman works with and manipulates and this that he must see, not the physical body we have become accustomed to looking at in order to pick up the cues (social or otherwise) as to who his client is. Gazing should therefore be practised by all shamans-in-training.

Starting simply, begin by sitting in front of a plant and allowing your gaze to go slightly out of focus so the plant becomes more background than foreground and, as you hold this way of looking, it could in fact be no more than a cut-out shape against the wall.

Once you have achieved this state of seeing start to explore the plant itself, again using almost peripheral vision, so you see how the leaves are composed of colour and light for example rather than solid form. Then start to see how the plant itself and each leaf has a glow around it, an aura of its own. This will prove useful as we move on to healing in later chapters.

Explorations

1. Rub your hands together to get your energy flowing, then hold them out before you to a distance of about 24 inches from your face, preferably in front of a plain dark background to ensure no distractions. Begin to gaze them, allowing your eyes to go slightly out of focus so you are aware of but not staring at your hands. Widen your fingers slowly and you will become aware of a 'smoke' between them which sticks to each finger as it is pulled apart. It may also appear as a ghostly outline. This is the energy body which surrounds you.

2. Experiment by asking a friend to stand in front of you against a dark background. Again allow your eyes to go slightly out of focus. Don't look directly at your friend but slightly past or above him (for some reason the energy body often seems clearer if you fix your gaze at a spot just between the shoulder and the top of the head, as if you are looking at something just over the person's shoulder). You will notice the same ghost image which is that person's energy body.

Sigils: Symbols of Power

A sigil is a picture made up of alphabetical letters or, rather, the lines and circles that comprise those letters. The word LOVE for example is composed of two vertical and four horizontal lines (in the L and the E), two angled lines (in the V) and a single circle (the O). The sigil itself is made by using these vertical and horizontal lines in L – O – V – E to create a shape, form or pattern that means something personal to you. By creating such a picture the shaman puts his intention and prayers into a form from which he can draw certain qualities (in this case of love) into his life which the sigil represents.

If he wishes to attract love for himself or a client, for example, he will begin by breaking the word down into its constituent lines and circles. There is no need to repeat any lines. So you will notice, for example, that the vertical in the L is replicated in the vertical of the E, as is the bottom horizontal of the L. Instead of using both the L and the E therefore, the E alone will suffice as this also incorporates the L and can stand for all of these lines.

The lines of the V and the O, however, are not repeated in any other letters so these need to be integrated separately into the drawing he makes. He might choose for example to connect the V to the base of the E and surround the whole with the circle of the O so that the word LOVE now becomes a sacred image, unrecognisable as a word but still carrying the energy of his intention to attract in the power of love.

Sigils can also be used to empower your space or your home by placing them there to attract the appropriate spiritual energy into your life. You can also carry them with you in order to remain focussed on your intent and maintain a connection to the spirits who can help with this. If you have the money to do so sigils can also be made into jewellery (such as a pendant or a broach) so you can wear them and allow their power to course through you.

Exploration

Meditate or journey on a particular quality or power you wish to attract into your life. Create a sigil for this.

Trance Postures

There are at least 80 different body postures now known, explored and their effects documented by the Cuyamungue Institute run by Felicitas Goodman and Belinda Gore, both of whom have written on the usage and purpose of these postures for journeying.

'Great beings who inhabit the realm of spirit that we call the Alternate Reality have been around for thousands of years, helping humans through our journeys here on Earth, and hunter-gatherer and horticultural peoples around the world have both documented their presence and preserved the means of access to them through their artwork on cave walls, in totem poles, in delicate gold or silver work, or in simple pottery. Their images have been perpetually in front of our eyes,' says Belinda Gore.

Even so, the true nature of these images was only redis-covered 40 years ago by anthropologist Felicitas Goodman whose findings suggest that the figures represented in this artwork are in fact ritual postures which enable ordinary people to enter non-ordinary consciousness and experience the spirit world. These postures produce a common effect because they all have one thing in common – the one thing we all share – the human body, the basic structure and functioning of which has remained unchanged since the time of our most ancient ancestors. The nervous and endocrine systems are in fact all much the same as they were 30,000 years ago, a fact which enables modern city dwellers to enter the Otherworld just as effectively through the same neural doorways as medicine men and shamans throughout history.

Dr Goodman identified several prerequisites for a successful trance experience:

1. The establishment of a sacred space – not necessarily a church, an altar or 'power place' but a place of sacred intent for the individual.
2. Participants must enter the trance state with the expectation of a sacred experience.
3. A repetitive sound must be used as an auditory cue to the nervous system to shift into non-ordinary reality. The rattle or drum is ideal and Dr Goodman confirms that a rhythm of about 200-220 beats per minute works best, which is consistent with other shamanic literature on the use of sound by tribal peoples.
4. A method for silencing the inner dialogue of the mind is essential. In her experiments Dr Goodman used simple meditative breathing.
5. The key factor, however, was that people need a shared approach to the exercise, a belief system to be part of, which acts to shape the trance state into a spiritual experience. The use of ritual body postures provided this common reference by overcoming individual and cultural differences. Trance postures worked for everyone irrespective of their worldview or belief systems. In the words of Belinda Gore, even 'Agnostic computer programmers could undergo a shamanic dismemberment during the fifteen minutes of an ecstatic trance session'.

Exploration

These are a few trance postures you can try for yourself to see what effects they produce (their actual purpose is given below).

Tattooed Jaguar

Kneel with legs spread so your knees form a 'V'. Cross your right big toe over the left big toe. Rest your buttocks on your heels and bend forward slightly at the waist. Curl your hands the amount needed to hold an imaginary medium-sized candle. Place your curled left hand palm down on your left knee and your right hand on your right knee, tilted upwards slightly (so if you were actually holding a candle, it would point at 45 degrees towards your other leg). Keep your elbows relaxed and slightly bow your arms. Face forward with your eyes closed.

Tennessee Diviner

Begin by kneeling, then raise your right knee and place your right foot sole down on the floor beside your left knee. Continue to kneel on your left knee, with your buttocks resting on this heel. Place your left hand palm down on the left knee and right hand palm down on the right knee, slightly to the left of your kneecap. Cock your head very slightly to the right as if wanting to look over your right knee. Keep your eyes closed and protrude your tongue a little between slightly parted lips.

Realm of the Dead

Stand with your feet parallel about 6 inches apart and point your toes straight ahead. Keep your knees slightly bent. Place your right hand over your waist with the ball of your hand covering your navel and your middle finger extending along the waistline. Your left arm is against your chest, with the palm of the hand against your chest so it is just above your right arm and parallel to it. Keep your upper arms relaxed and close to your body. Face forward with your eyes closed.

The Tattooed Jaguar, dated from around 1,400 BC, is considered a shapeshifting posture which facilitates a view of reality from the perspective of a big cat. In Gore's words 'many individuals become sensitised to the non-human world and grow in rapport with the animals'. Is this what you experienced?

The Tennessee Diviner, dating from around AD 700, is a divinatory posture which puts users in touch with a spirit with a penchant for offering advice on ritual. The spirit contacted can be 'short tempered, brief and even cryptic' but 'generous with exacting details' concerning specific healing rituals.

The Realm of the Dead posture, from fifth century BC Germany, mediates journeys to the middle world. 'The traveller wanders in desolate areas... but eventually something changes and the journeyer begins to rise into a new form and a new life'. From your previous journeys to the middle world, perhaps this posture produced a mood in you that was familiar?

It seems clear from the experiences of those who use trance postures that they do produce qualitatively different journeys and that each trance posture is different in itself from others. Postures by their very nature seem to open a specific doorway to a particular Otherworld territory or state of being.

Quick Test 3

Without looking back over this chapter, how might a shaman use the following in healing work:

1. Smudge
2. Power songs and chants
3. Plant spirit medicine

Exercises

Continue to practice your journeying, your dream journal work and work your way through the explorations in this chapter. Before you read on please also undertake these next pieces of work which have a bearing on the subjects we will look at in upcoming chapters.

Exercise 1: The Spirit of the Drum

The drum is composed of wood and skin – plant and animal – both of which gave their lives so you might have this healing tool. Make a journey to the spirits of the animal and the tree within your drum and ask them why they offered themselves in this way and what their sacred purpose is or was.

Exercise 2: Other Tools

From the tools you have read about and explored you will have formed an affinity for one or two in particular. Which of the shaman's tools particularly call to you and why? From your explorations with these tools what else have you learned about them?

Four

Healing the Energy Body

In this Chapter

The nature and theory of illness in shamanism, the nature of the soul, spirit intrusions and spirit extraction, purifying and empowering the healing space, matrix energy, repairing the energy body.

Reading for this Chapter

The Sin Eater's Last Confessions (Ross Heaven) contains first-hand accounts of healing, especially within the Celtic tradition; *Plant Spirit Wisdom* (Ross Heaven) describes methods of healing. Other books referred to include *The Way of the Shaman* by Michael Harner.

Equipment Required

Drum or drumming tape
Rattle
Pendulum and crystals or stones

The Nature and Theory of Illness

Shamanic healing has a different view of the nature and causes of disease than orthodox Western medicine. The latter tends to intervene at the point where the disease has become visible but rarely addresses the underlying cause. Shamanism, on the other hand, aims to intervene at the point of the cause so the underlying issues are dealt with.

For the shaman, there are a number of ways in which disease might arise but in every case there is an unseen world where all illness comes from and from where it can migrate to the physical plane as a result of magical or spiritual actions or distress. In this belief system disease will always manifest along these lines:

(4) Physical (the seen world)

▲

(3) Mental

▲

(2) Emotional

▲

(1) Spiritual (the unseen world)

All of these – the spiritual, emotional, mental and physical – are different 'bodies' or aspects of the self that each of us have. Together they make up the energy body or soul.

That stratum of the energy body which comprises the spiritual self is furthest away from our physical body, beginning at a distance of about an arm's length from us and stretching into infinity (although its impact and effects on the world around us gets weaker the further it gets from us). The emotional self is slightly closer, in a band about eighteen inches thick which begins about twelve inches from the physical body. The mental self is the space between the emotional and physical bodies.

The Progression of Disease

At the root of every illness is a problem that stems from the unseen (spirit) world and affects our spiritual bodies first. Depending on how in tune we are with spirit we may or may not notice that something is happening to us as the illness begins to connect with our energy field.

As the illness migrates towards the physical body the problem will become more noticeable and start to make an impact on our lives. It will be registered next by the emotions. If we are in tune with our feelings we may sense that there is something 'not quite right' with us although we may still be unable to articulate what the problem is or what we are really feeling. As the illness becomes more solid and physical we will become increasingly aware that something is wrong. At this point the illness is entering the mental self and the mind goes to work on the problem so we may become consciously aware of some event that haunts us and seems to have a connection to our feelings and illness. Or perhaps our mind also becomes affected by the spiritual fallout from that event, in which case mental illness, anxiety, depression and so on might result. Finally, the spiritual issue will create a physical problem.

Stress is a modern example. There is no such thing as 'A Stress' (in fact, the term was only invented less than 100 years ago). You cannot examine one in the way you can a broken leg for example; it exists in the world of the unseen; it is a mood, a sense, a feeling – a spirit (of the workplace, a relationship or a life circumstance for example). Yet many of us are affected by stress emotionally and mentally, leading to relationship problems, mental anguish, anger, panic attacks and depression. Eventually, when our coping strategies run out and our emotional and mental selves cannot deal with it any longer stress begins assaulting the body and is nowadays recognised even by orthodox medical professionals as a contributor to cancers, strokes, ulcers, heart attacks, high blood pressure and many other physical problems as well as numerous associated ones, such as increased smoking, drinking and eating disorders and decreased sex drive and life force. Stress is the invisible world making itself felt on the visible.

Because all illness has a spiritual cause in this way the shaman believes first and foremost that its cure also lies in the spiritual domain. There may be many ways in which these spiritual problems arise, however, and to understand them and their cures the shaman must also know the workings of the soul since this (the spiritual) is the part of us that is always first attacked.

The Soul

Socrates wrote that, 'The cure of the part should not be attempted without treatment of the whole. No attempt should be made to cure the body without the Soul. Let no one persuade you to cure the mind until he has first given you his Spirit. For the great error of our day is that physicians separate the heart from the mind and the mind from the body.'

The scientific and medical community is sceptical about the idea of a soul since it cannot be seen, quantified, analysed or measured in the way of the physical sciences. But even the most hardened sceptic might concede that most of what we think of as 'solid' around us is actually bits of solid material held together by energetic forces. The discoveries of atomic and quantum physics have taught us that much.

Scientists are used to manipulating this energy in laboratories and research establishments where they too are dealing with the unseen world. Only the terminology is different. The shaman calls this energy 'soul' but his approach is in many ways the same as the scientist – both are manipulating forces that are invisible to the naked eye to create a material effect in the visible world.

Because he is an expert in the nature and workings of the soul, the shaman is aware of its subtleties and flow. In fact he may even conceive of these subtleties as a number of different souls, not just one. The Shipibo Indians of the Amazon, for example, believe that every part of the human body and every organ has its own soul. Others believe that the soul exists in the blood and so permeates the entire human body, infusing each part with its own different life force.

To use the Haitian tradition as an example, here it is believed that the soul is comprised of three parts – three different types of energy – known as the gros bon anje ('big good angel'), ti bon anje ('little good angel') and the met tete ('master of the head').

The gros bon anje is the place within our soul that resonates with the God-energy of the universe. If we are decent people, in good relationship to God, then this part of our soul is protected and we are filled with power. This bears some similarity to the sin eating (shamanic healing) tradition of the Celts: i.e. if our souls are pure we are 'in our power' and protected from illness and harm; it is 'the weights on the soul' (the things we have done wrong, our 'sins') which lead to illness.

The met tete represents a connection both within and without us to a specific guardian angel who is our 'father' or 'mother' and under whose protection we were born. Again, many shamanic cultures share this belief although they may tend to conceive of the guardian spirit in animal rather than human or angel-like form. The Yakuts of Siberia, for example, say that an animal takes a part of the human soul under its protection at birth and in this way ensures that its human relation can never die from a magical attack since his entire soul is never present to be damaged. In Nigeria there is a similar belief and a person will unite during initiation with a particular wild animal that becomes the protector of his soul. During the initiation rite this person and the animal swap blood, becoming 'blood brothers' as the human inoculates the chosen animal with his own blood and then drinks an amount of blood from a cut made to the animal's ear. In this way they are bonded for life and the death of one will result in the death of the other. They therefore have a vested interest in caring for each other and treating their complementary species with respect.

The ti bon anje is the spirit of man within normal life and therefore open to damage and attack from the spiritual and other dangers of this world and from the desires of people who wish to take our power to satisfy their neediness and greed for more.

The ti bon anje is a moral principle for appropriate living. If a man is in good relationship to his community and to others around him he will be well and the community will reward him with love, companionship and protection. If he acts selfishly or immorally, however, the community will cast him out and he becomes vulnerable and unloved.

With the decline of religion in the West most of us do not have a good relationship with God; many of us do not even believe in God any more since we have never been given direct evidence of God by our priests. And even if we are church-goers orthodox religion does not teach us to develop a connection with a particular angel or guardian, leaving us exposed in our souls at the level of the gros bon anje and the met tete, which are ways of energetic interaction with the world. Our energies become depleted since we have no battery from which to recharge them and once we are powerless it is easier for our spirits to be attacked or even stolen. We end up depressed and dis-spirited, two of the most frequent complaints in the modern West where tranquillisers and anti-depressants are now the most prescribed drugs.

Moreover, through the decline of Western community we have little protection at the level of the ti bon anje and many of us feel isolated, alone and unloved, leading to self-doubt and anxiety. Such stresses (as we have seen) can lead to physical illnesses.

In shamanic terms these feelings of aloneness, disconnection and disempowerment (or the illnesses that come from them) may be seen as spirit intrusions. When we feel powerless we cannot defend against the spiritual forces of the universe and so our bodies become open to attack from entities that are energetically out of resonance with us. This is one of the classical means for the spread of disease.

Intrusions

Spirit intrusions are power intrusions. As Michael Harner puts it: 'They are not natural to the body, but are brought in. If you are power-full, you will resist them. Thus possession of guardian spirit power is fundamental to health. Serious illness is usually only possible when a person is dis-spirited, has lost this energizing force, the guardian spirit. When a person becomes depressed, weak, prone to illness, it is a symptom that he has lost his power... and thus can no longer resist, or ward off the unwanted 'infections' or intrusions.'

In shamanic terms, the intrusion that invades you begins its existence as energy but soon develops an awareness of life and the will to live, becoming more and more physical as it does so. If this drive-to-life is stronger than your drive to resist it, it will eventually develop an independent material presence, fuelling itself by drawing from your energy so that to all intents and purposes it possesses you.

This is not as fantastical as it sounds. Indeed, science offers some support for this traditional view. In a number of experiments it has been shown that people who are weaker and less power-filled are also less resistant to disease. The psychologists Holmes and Rahe found for example that the most stressful life events – those which bring us down, depress us or leave us in a weakened state – such as bereavement, divorce, a change of job, redundancy, retirement, etc – *always* correlate with the onset of illness. In one experiment two groups of people – those under stress and those with a non-stressful life – were asked to inhale a common cold virus. Those who were stressed caught colds within days while those who were happy with their lives and sure of themselves did not get ill. Another experiment showed that people under stress always develop throat infections when a virus is circulating and consistently do so within four days of exposure to it.

What modern science is acknowledging in such studies is almost a latent endorsement of the shaman's view that being power-full will prevent disease and ward off spiritual attack while emotional and spiritual weakness gives the disease the foothold it needs.

When physical illness does result, therefore, it will rarely be the shaman's primary (or at least not his only) concern since he knows that by dealing with the point of origination and the cause of the disease (the intrusive spirit and the circumstances that admitted it) he will also heal its manifestations in the emotional, mental and physical bodies. The most important thing then, is to extract the harmful spirit (or damaging energy) from the energy body of the client. When this is done the client's energy body will reconstitute itself to close the gap left by the intrusion and his power will begin to circulate again.

Spirit Extraction

The method of spirit extraction is consistent across many cultures. Usually it involves finding a replacement host for the spirit of the disease so it can be removed from the client's body.

Last chapter we looked at the use of eggs to provide a host receptacle for this spirit. In India by contrast the patient is brushed with leaves and branches so that the wood absorbs the spiritual poison. In Timor fatigue is cured by fanning oneself with leaves which are then thrown away so that the tiredness goes with them while in the Solomon Islands the same problem is relieved by rubbing oneself with stones which are then cast into the ocean. Among the Baganda sickness is cured by the medicine man making a model of his patient from clay or plantain which is then buried. The model represents the 'diseased' persona and once it is gone the true persona (or disease-free client) can emerge and the patient can get back his life. In these cases, the new hosts for the disease are the leaves, stones, plantain and earth respectively.

In some cultures animals are used as the host so that the illness is transferred to them. In Morocco, for example, evil spirits are removed by the medicine man and cast into the bodies of wild boar, while in South Africa a patient will confess his sins to the medicine man in the presence of a goat which absorbs the sickness caused by his immorality. The goat is then set loose in an unoccupied part of the veldt and the illness is lost in the desert (there is a similarity here to the Bible story of Aaron confessing the 'sins of Israel' before a goat that was also sent out into the desert to die). In Welsh tradition sin eaters were employed at funerals to fulfil a similar purpose by eating a meal of bread and salt from the belly of the deceased thus absorbing their sins and ensuring a safe passage for the dead person to the afterlife.

Extraction is not just a mechanical process, however, whereby touching the patient with another host will deactivate the illness. Before the shaman does anything at all he must ensure that he is completely power-filled himself since spirit intrusions are also energy forms and, like lightning or electricity, will find the path of least resistance. If the shaman is weaker than the intrusion he is removing he will absorb the illness himself.

Thus, it is common for the shaman to use song, dance, chanting, drumming or other methods to create the power in himself that he needs before he begins any treatment of another – and this is something you should also do. *This focus on self-empowerment, followed by the intention to heal, is the first step in any shamanic medicine. Only then should the spirit intrusion be addressed directly.* It is also necessary before the healing begins to assemble the tools of extraction work which you, the healer, will use. In modern practice this might mean the following:

- A blanket and pillows for the client to lie down on
- A long feather or a number of smaller ones bound together to create a 'knife-like' shape and length
- A smudge stick and a holder for this
- A rattle
- A drum or drumming tape
- A pendulum
- At least four quartz crystals or stones

The healing then proceeds in the following stages.

1. Filling Yourself with Power

Find the method that works best for you so you become filled with energy and in your power. Many shamans drum for a while until they feel uplifted, strong and full of energy. During this ritual they also journey to their power animals, guides and guardian spirits to call them in and enlist their aid in healing and protection during what is to come.

2. Purifying and Empowering the Healing Space

The healing ritual begins with some form of smudging to purify the client and healer, the room and the healing tools. A smudge stick might be used or in other cultures (e.g. Peru, Haiti) tobacco smoke or rum might be sprayed around the room.

As he does this the healer will continue to fill his own body with power, perhaps drumming or singing so he deepens further into a trance-like state and strengthens his connection to his allies and the natural forces or elements that will eventually take the spirit intrusion on his behalf – whether this is a tree, a field, a mountain, the wind or the sea (see chapter two – Nature Allies).

During this period of connection with the spirits some healers also call on the powers of the Four Directions which broadly correspond to the qualities of the medicine wheels used by many shamanic traditions around the world:

- *East* is where all life begins. It is the place of passion, the spirit of infancy, the innocence and strength of the newborn, the sense of purity, of physicality and the element of Fire.
- *South* is the direction of becoming, of childhood and young adulthood, the emotions and the element of Water.
- *West* is the direction of mature reason and the adult, the rational mind, the sense of perspective, the element of Air.
- *North* is where physical life ends and rebirth to the East

begins. It is the place of the wise Elder, of reconnection to the unseen world of spirit, of mature informed reflection and the element of Earth.

All of the elements are addressed in this petition – Fire, Water, Air and Earth – as well as the guardians of the various bodies that make up the soul of the client – physical, emotional, mental and spiritual. You are therefore bringing the most potent forces in the universe to bear on the healing of your client.

3. Creating a Protective Matrix

Having followed these initial procedures the healer will then ask the client to lie down and relax while he invokes a matrix of energy with lines coming down from the sky to each of the Four Directions, the four points of the compass, to form a pyramid of protection around her. He then visualises a pyramid of the same energy from below her, up from the Earth, to link again with the Four Directions. The client is then held at the centre of a diamond of energetic power.

This is important since you are about to work with her soul and the spirits – all spirits – are aware of this. The force of intention in creating this protective diamond ensures that you do not get any uninvited guests during the healing you are about to perform! (Not that these spirits may necessarily be harmful to you or your client, but uninterrupted focus and attention as well as intention is important in healing so you do not want any distractions).

The words you use to call in or invoke these powers are best drawn from the poetry of your own soul. In this way they are heartfelt and carry your serious intention for healing.

Once this preparatory work is done the next task of the healer is to find out the state of health of the client's energy body.

4. Repairing the Energy Body

A healthy human energy body has an egg-like shape which surrounds the physical body (and also runs through it) to a distance of about an arm's length in all directions. This egg holds all of the energy that is us throughout our lives.

The energy body is weakened by the onset of disease so that rather than resembling a healthy cocoon around the physical body it will be knocked out of shape and may also be spread very thinly. If the energy body has been damaged in this way it must first be restored to its natural shape so that the client has access to her power in the configuration that is most effective for her to make use of it.

There are also areas of peak energetic activity within this field. In Eastern medicines such as acupuncture these are known as meridians. Along them are the chakra points. Chakra is the Sanskrit word for wheel since this is what these areas look like: small spiralling wheels of light which are areas of power in the veins that carry energy around the body. They are most pronounced at the crown, forehead (the 'third eye'), throat, heart, solar plexus, perineum and at the soles of the feet (the base of the body) and in a healthy human being spin in a circular clockwise direction which is the direction of all good energy.

The chakras also connect in the physical body to the major organs and important parts of the endocrine system. Thus, an energy disturbance within the chakras may often suggest an existing or emerging problem in the client's physical body.

Knowledge of the chakras can therefore be useful to us as healers since each is associated with a spiritual, emotional or mental concern and with a physical state or problem. The following is a list of associations for each. This should not be treated as 'gospel' but can be used as one diagnostic tool.

- *Crown.* Concerned with issues of faith, hope, personal belief and connections to the divine and the infinite.

Physical problems associated with this chakra (i.e. when energy is not circulating correctly or effectively within it) include depression, extreme tiredness, muscular or skeletal pain and skin problems.

- *Third Eye.* Issues concerning consciousness, reason and the ability to see our real/spiritual place in the world. Issues of 'lostness' and lack of connection to others can also be involved here. Physically these issues may give rise to problems with the eyes, ears, nose, brain or nervous system.

- *Throat.* Issues of truth and the inability to 'speak our mind' or 'say our piece' to release the emotions within us. Physically these issues may result in throat and neck problems or diseases associated with the mouth, oesophagus, teeth or gums.

- *Heart.* Issues concerning the emotions, which may be either 'positive' (love, compassion, empathy, forgiveness, etc) or 'negative' (anger, jealousy, control issues, hatred, etc). Physically issues at the heart chakra may also affect the lungs, breasts, shoulders, arms or the heart and blood system.

- *Solar Plexus.* Issues of self-esteem, self-worth and personal power. This is the seat of the will and of 'making things happen', of putting ourselves forward in life, walking our talk and choosing our path with heart. Physically, blockages in the energy system here may lead to problems with the stomach, liver, kidneys, adrenal glands or spleen.

- *Perineum.* Issues of security and personal relationships, usually involving a power exchange of some kind. Physically these may lead to intestinal or bladder disorders or problems with the sex organs, pelvis or hips.

- *Soles of the feet.* Issues of 'grounding', 'under-standing', balance, our (normally socially-conditioned) beliefs about ourselves and the relationship patterns we attract into our lives. Physically, issues at this chakra can lead to back or leg problems or a weakening of the immune system. Emotionally they are implicated in a client's inability to move forward in life and may manifest as a sense of being stuck or caught up in old habits.

Before dealing with the chakras, however, the energy body as a whole must be re-aligned.

5. Energy Realignment

The use of a pendulum and crystals will reveal the shape of the energy body to you. Hold the pendulum over your client and work your way out to the Four Directions of her body. At first the pendulum will be still but it will start to move when it reaches the boundary of her energy body.

In normal circumstances of power and good health this will be an arm's length from her physical body but in situations of illness and spiritual damage might only be a few inches, a few feet or, indeed, some yards away. Wherever you reach this boundary, place one of your crystals there to mark it. Continue around her body until all of the directions are covered. You will then be left with an energy map made up of crystals that now surround your client.

Small stones may also be used instead of (or as well as) crystals. However you mark the energy body – with crystals, stones or both – the map you create will tell you where your client's energy is located and where it needs to be moved to and from bearing in mind that the energy body should only be a few feet away from her physical body and should normally have an egg-like shape.

If the energy body is too far away from where it should be, use your hands to feel for it (you will often experience a temperature difference at the boundary or your hands may shake or tingle) then push it back (or use a feather to waft it back) to where it needs to be. Use the pendulum again to check that it has moved and reposition the crystals to map its new location.

7. Repairing the Chakras

Now hold the pendulum over each of her chakras in turn and note if these are energised and spinning in the right (clockwise) direction. If they are, the pendulum will also spin that way. If it is immobile, moves to and fro or spins in the wrong (anti-clockwise) direction the chakra will need to be repaired.

This is done by pushing the palm of your hand down into the client's energy field at the relevant chakra point and moving it in a clockwise direction, like turning a wheel, with the intention of moving the energy in the right direction.

If the chakra is not spinning correctly even after these rotations it may be because it is clogged. Our chakras are the mouths of the energy body and just like our physical mouths can become choked if there is too much (spiritual, emotional – or literal) pollution around us.

The solution is to dip your fingers into the chakra (it will feel like going against the current in a small whirlpool or eddy or like a cool breeze on your fingers) and pull out the stuff – the build-up of energy pollution – that is blocking it. Blow it away from your fingers to the safe-keeping of the allies you have made in Nature, visualising it clearly as it is sucked towards and then taken in by the mountain or lake or tree that is your healing partner in the middle world, where this energy will be absorbed and neutralised. When you dip your fingers into the chakra again it should feel warmer than before, signalling that this pollution has indeed been removed. Now spin up the chakra again, using your hand in the same way as before.

Once you have done all of the above your client will have a properly aligned energy body, which also makes it easier for you to see any intrusions within it that need to be removed. It is then time to move on to the next two processes that may be necessary in shamanic healing – spirit extraction (the removal of intrusions) and soul or power retrieval, the return of good energy. We look at these in the next chapter.

Quick Test 4

1. Why and how is illness created according to shamanic thinking?
2. What do we mean by the term 'energy body'?
3. What is the 'ti bon anje' and why is it important to take care with this part of our energy?
4. What is a spirit intrusion?

Exercises

Continue to practice your journeying and dream work. Before you look at the next chapter please also undertake these pieces of work.

Exercise 1: Connecting with Power

Calling in power is vital before any healing work begins. Say why and describe the method/s you use to empower yourself and fill up with energy. What do you do? How does this change you? How do you feel after calling in power?

Exercise 2: Mapping the Energy Body

Practice on a friend the use of crystals and/or stones to map the energy body. Use a pendulum to find her energy field and then use your hands to make any adjustments to the energy body and clean out the chakras if necessary. Pay attention to your friend's observations of how this felt to her as well and any changes she noticed. This is useful feedback and a validation of your work.

Five

Spirit Extraction and Soul Retrieval

In this Chapter

Spirit extraction, restoring power, when the soul is lost, a framework for healing, healing yourself, the power of confession, retrieving the soul through warriorship.

Suggested Reading

The Sin Eater's Last Confessions (Ross Heaven), *Shamanism* (Mircea Eliade).

Equipment Required

Drum or drumming tape

Rattle

Eggs, feathers and other medicine tools referred to in the text (optional). Also refer back to chapter three to revise how these tools might be used

Spirit Extraction: Removing Negative Energies

During your work on the client's energy body (see last chapter) you may have become aware of some form of energy that seemed out of resonance with her own, that you sensed should not be there or feel is not helpful or healthy for her. In shamanic terms this is an intrusive spirit that needs to be removed. If your client is expressing feelings of confusion, tiredness, fatigue or talks of being drained, unclear or not having the energy to get things done this can also be an indicator of spirit intrusion because the entity she is carrying is feeding from her energy, leaving her depleted.

Spirit intrusions are 'negative' energies (in the sense that they are unhelpful or out of resonance with the client's own energy system not that they are necessarily 'evil') that have become attached to her spirit. In effect she has an infection, a virus or a parasite that is draining energy from her to sustain itself.

Such energies *might* have been sent deliberately by someone who wants power over her. In Peru for example there is a practice of directing magical darts known as *virote* into the energy system of an enemy, where they take physical form and begin to work against the body. A virote, given enough time to establish itself and take power from a person, can become so strong that it turns into a physical illness or problem. In Haiti there is a similar practice where dead spirits are sent to attack a person. This is called *expedition mort* ('sending the dead'). In Australia there is a trance posture for this sort of action, called Bone Pointing where the magician uses a hollow bone to focus negative energies and send them as if fired from the barrel of a gun into the body of a rival. In Africa a simple seed or stone, charged with negativity, might be buried in the Earth so that when the target steps over it the destructive energy it contains will leap into his body.

In the modern West such practices are uncommon and it is rare indeed that a shamanic practitioner will ever see a case of genuine 'cursing' or spiritual attack (although it could happen). In the dance of office politics and the power plays of love affairs and daily rivalries, however, such negative energies often do get sent, sometimes deliberately (in the sense of wishing harm or bad luck to a person), but usually sometimes unconsciously and unwittingly. Explosions of rage, 'acting out' of personal issues, or the projection of bad feelings onto others are all forms that such an energetic attack might take. When we use expressions like 'she stabbed me in the back', 'he was looking daggers' or 'if looks could kill', on some level we are accepting the reality that not only do we send such negative forces out into the world but they can have deeply damaging effects on the person who receives them.

Spirit intrusions can also become attached to us without conscious intent by the sender. The feeling of being 'haunted' by an ex-lover, for example, probably suggests that there is still an energy connection between you and while this exists you will be living in a past you are unable to forget. In this way you are also giving away power by living for someone who no longer exists in your life except as a memory (i.e. in energetic form).

If you believe that any of these situations may be true for your client you should check her energy body for intrusive presences. To do this you journey to the spirit world in the way you have done before but this time your intention is not to enter the upper or lower worlds but the energy body of your client to see if there is an attachment to be removed and if so, where it is. (Technically then this is a middle world journey). (Again, don't practice this yet; just read the instructions for the technique).

Seeing and Removing Intrusions

With your eyes closed or only slightly open, scan your client's energy body (refer back to the exercises on gazing), seeing and sensing any differences in colour or texture and allowing yourself to become aware at these places of any entities that are attached to them. The spirits that work with us will ensure that these are very visible to us by making them appear in a form that we personally find distasteful. Black tar, swarming insects, snakes and reptiles are common examples. *This does not mean that these things actually exist in a physical form within the client's body!* It means, rather, that your spirits have shown them to you in this way so you will not miss the place where this energy is rooted.

Do not, under any circumstances therefore suggest to your client that such a creature is actually a part of her! (In America a psychotherapist who used this shamanic technique on a client and told her that she saw a rat inside her – instead of phrasing it more subtly as 'an unhelpful energy' for example – was successfully sued by the client and had to pay compensation for the distress her remark had apparently caused. Remember that law courts are not normally on the side of alternative medicine but exist to support the status quo, including the orthodox medical system).

Once you see the intrusion ask for confirmation from the spirits who are working with you and if they are in agreement with your diagnosis get down next to that part of your client's body where the intrusion is localised, so you are face-to-face with it. As repulsive as this entity may appear to you it too has a right to life and to a fair chance to act honourably, so talk to it (telepathically if you prefer not to speak out loud). Reason, negotiate, explain the bigger picture that the intrusion can't see – that it is part of a living organism (your client) that is suffering because of its presence and ask it if it is prepared to leave peacefully and willingly.

If it is, your side of the bargain is to provide it with a new home. Eggs are often used for this (see chapter three) but stones and feathers offer an alternative solution. In the Otherworld, the energetic parallel of our own, simple objects such as feathers take on a healing power that is as precise and effective as a surgeon's blade. The feather, dipped into your client's energy body, will pull the intrusion towards it and you can then use the sharp edge of the feather to cut it away from the client. The feather will absorb it.

Your intent and powers of spiritual seeing (gazing) are important here too. As you focus on the feather, *see* the intrusion moving into it. *Intend* that this will happen and maintain this focus until all traces of the intrusion are gone. Your client's face is a good indicator that the intrusion has been removed. She will feel younger, lighter, less troubled when she is free of it and her face and body will reflect this.

You can then either blow the intrusive spirit away from the feather to the safe-keeping of the ally you have made in Nature or dispose of it in an honourable and respectful way by taking the feather that now contains it to a safe place and burying it where others are unlikely to find it. Offer a gift of thanks to the Earth and to the feather for agreeing to take this energy away and discharge it back to Nature. Offerings such as tobacco, rum or corn are usually acceptable.

If the intrusion refuses to leave, however, you will need to get tough. While it is true that all things are alive and deserve our respect, you are here to work for your client not on behalf of the intrusion.

One classical method for establishing authority over recalcitrant intrusions is to rattle at or near the intrusion, which has the affect of agitating it and loosening its grip on the client's body. You can then use the feather to scoop it up and dispose of it in the same way as above or grab the intrusion with your hands and blow it to your Nature ally.

Cleaning the Wound

Once the intrusion is gone your client will be left with a sensitive patch in her energy field where a piece of energy is now missing, just like a wound to the physical body. It is important to apply a spiritual 'antiseptic' to this, as you would to any wound in order to clean and protect it. One method is to blow Florida Water over the area. Florida Water is a perfume made from plants which are held in alcohol. Its name in Peru is Agua Florida which is an indication of its use – it is 'flourishing or flowering water' which helps the client heal and attract good energies into her life so her luck is changed and she may flourish and grow strong. It is administered to the wound by taking a mouthful of it and then spraying it over the client's energy (and physical) body, a process known as *soplada*.

Florida Water is usually available from botanicas (spiritual healing stores) but can be bought from web suppliers too. (There is also a recipe for making your own in my book *Vodou Shaman*). As an alternative you can smudge your client with sage or sprinkle mineral water over the sensitive area instead. Water may work just as well, however, since, as with all shamanic healing, it is the *intention* to heal that really produces results.

Restoring Power

Understandably, since the intrusion has been feeding off your client's energy, part of her power will have been taken from her by this entity and most shamans will now wish to carry out a healing to undo the damage caused by the intrusive spirit and fill the void in the energy body caused by the extraction. This healing is known as power retrieval (also see chapter two) and its aim is to return useful energy to the client.

The fundamental procedure for power retrieval is the same as you undertook for yourself when you brought back a power animal from the lower world. This procedure is to:

- Journey to the lower world with the intention of finding an animal ally as a source of power for your client
- Look for running water and trace it back to its source
- There you will find an animal waiting for you that has answered the call of your intention
- Ask the animal for any advice or information your client needs to make her healing more effective
- Then gather the animal in your arms and return with it, retracing your steps back to the room where your client is. The animal now changes form and becomes, in ordinary reality, helpful energy or spirit
- Placing your hands on your client's solar plexus and cupping them, blow sharply through them so this energy is pushed into her body. Repeat this a few times if need be until you clearly see that this energy has been absorbed
- Repeat this process at the crown of her head
- Finally, rattle around her body four times to seal this energy in

Allies from Nature

In almost exactly the same way it is possible to connect your client with a spirit ally from Nature. Since Nature is the energetic parallel of our own world this is helpful in giving her a source of strength that is not just spiritual but also exists in material reality so she can physically visit it too and draw strength and sustenance from it.

Journey as before to natural features of the middle world (see chapter one), all of which are alive with spirit, and ask if they have a gift of power for your client. If the answer is 'no' move on and find one that does. If the answer is 'yes' gather this energy in your arms and then find another and another – three is enough – before returning to your client. You can if you wish visualise this as taking a walk in Nature and allowing yourself to be drawn to various natural forms such as trees or lakes, mountains or clouds, each of which has energy it may offer your client.

Blow these gifts of power into her solar plexus and crown as before, reciting (out loud if you wish) what it is that you have returned. For example:

Power of moon I return to you
[Blow]
Power of sun I return to you
[Blow]
Power of rain I return to you
[Blow]
Then rattle around her body to seal in the energy.

Counselling

When you have completed the power retrieval your client will need to understand a little about what you have done for her and how she can maintain her new energy and the connection you have opened for her to spirit.

Unless your client has approached you specifically for

shamanic healing and is familiar with its concepts and processes, it is often better to talk in general terms. Suggest perhaps that you have helped her to establish a connection with a guardian angel or a loving guide who wants to look out for her, and that she makes an offering to this angel or guide in thanks for its help. Or tell her that she can enhance her healing and strengthen her connection to the powers of Nature by finding something in the material world that represents the natural force you have returned. Encourage her to put up a picture of the moon above her bed, for example, or to light a candle representing the power of the sun, or provide her with the recipe for a herbal bath she can take (see chapter eight) which will help her heal and connect with the power of water. Or simply suggest that she spends some time walking in Nature where she is likely to be exposed to these forces anyway.

In a way similar to how a modern Western psychotherapist might work with symbols, it can also be useful to discuss what you have seen. If you have returned a power animal in the form of horse or a fox, for example, ask your client what these animals mean *to her*. What useful, healing or empowering qualities do they have, for example, which she may make use of or learn from in her life – and draw upon too as energetic strengths since they are now a part of her (e.g. a horse, *as a symbol*, may mean 'endurance' while a fox may mean 'cunning', in the sense of intuition and intelligence).

By the same token the sun and moon have qualities associated with them too. Never assume that what *you* think they mean (or even the stereotypes we associate with them – e.g. sun/masculine; moon/feminine) are the same for your client, however, (e.g. in some countries the moon is a masculine symbol, or it may mean something totally different to the person you are working on, such as 'brightness' or 'romance' rather than 'feminine'). What this symbol means *to your client* is always more important and by asking her to tell you, you will also be assisting her to connect with these energies so they become allies to her immediately.

Completing the Work

When your client leaves or as the healing ceremony ends, close the sacred space you have created and release your helping spirits. A simple way of doing this is to blow out your candle if you have been using one, put out any incense you are using and then clap your hands three times, offering words of thanks and farewell until the next time you work with your spirits.

Exploration

Find a volunteer you can work with to explore the methods of spirit extraction and power return. In normal circumstances I would not recommend that you work with friends or family but you can do so for the purposes of this practice. Be careful, however, that what you know of them already does not influence your judgement of their need for extraction or retrieval and that what you learn of them through the healing does not affect your relationship with them.

When the Soul is Lost

We all have an amount of energy within us which is the totality of our soul. In cases of power loss some of this energy has been removed from us through the impact of life or the specific actions of others but this can normally be returned through power retrieval (see above). With soul loss, however, so much energy has been taken from us that we may feel extreme depletion and have little hope of recovery without the intervention of a healer.

In the case of an abused child, for example, the loss of power will occur daily as a result of the physical and mental suffering that takes place. If that child is removed from the abusive family and taken into care where it is loved and supported, research shows that the power she has lost may return over time. Where the abuse is constant and there is no intervention, however, the soul will continue to be ground away.

In the psychological literature we sadly read of many such cases. In the 1970s, for example, twin seven-year-old boys were discovered in a cellar in Czechoslovakia where they had been imprisoned for more than five years by their stepmother. Neither of the boys could walk or talk, both were suffering from rickets and they were both extremely fearful. Despite their trauma, hospitalisation and fostering into loving families enabled the boys to recover. By removing them from the abusive situation and providing the love they needed for their souls to heal they were eventually returned to power.

Genie, on the other hand, was found when she was thirteen, chained in an attic and punished by her father if she made any sound. When discovered, she had the physical development of a six year old and was described as 'unsocialised, primitive and hardly human'. She could make barely any sounds and could not walk.

Genie was also hospitalised and fostered but in her case she went to a family where she was further abused and then to new foster parents who separated and divorced so she was never able to experience a secure environment where she felt loved and able to restore her power. Nor was she ever able to adjust to social life or develop language. She remained 'hardly human'.

Immoral actions like this may lead to the soul's withdrawal from the world. This is known as soul loss – or, indeed, may even go beyond soul loss into the area known as soul theft, where somebody seemingly wishes to deliberately steal the power of another person entirely, no matter what the damage to that person. Such situations are doubly tragic because the thief has often been abused and drained of power him or herself through some trauma in their own lives. That is why they are inclined to steal power from another in the first place, almost as a survival function. The real tragedy is that they can never actually use this power because it is out of resonance with their own, so in these situations nobody wins.

Another way in which the soul may be damaged is in moments of great shock or pain or at times of chronic illness or great fear. When soul fragments leave the body for any of these reasons, like all energy they follow the path of least resistance and so will take flight to that part of the Otherworld that is easiest for them to reach: the spiritual middle world.

Lost soul parts are often drawn to the energy of natural features and especially to trees and water which are the gateways to other worlds. In the Congo, for example, when the soul of a sick man leaves his body the medicine man will track it to a tree where it is hiding. A branch of the tree must then be broken off and carried back to the village where the sick person lies. This branch is laid next to the patient and the medicine man will then perform a ritual to transfer the soul back to its owner. A similar soul-hunt is performed by the Batak people of Sumatra who chase the soul through the natural world, chanting for it to return from where it is 'lingering in the wood, or on the hills, or in the dale'.

Why are these souls drawn to nature and to trees? Because, just as in the symbolism of the world tree, trees link all of the worlds. The lost soul longs for love and community, for return to a simpler world, and it is here at these gateways between the dimensions that it is likely to find what it most yearns for.

All the time it remains in the presence of these gateways the soul is vulnerable, however, since the spirits may indeed take pity on it and open the doorway between worlds to accept it back into their community. At the same time the soul lost in the middle world is vulnerable to attack from confused or unevolved spirits.

Bringing Back the Soul

The first action of the shaman must be to establish how and why these soul parts were lost. Sometimes the client has a clear sense of this and can tell you (or at least hint at) the reasons. She may explicitly mention an abusive relationship, a tragic love affair, a divorce, an accident or a family tragedy, for example. Some clients, however, have little awareness of the cause of their problems but can only tell you that they feel 'stuck' or 'lost'. In these cases the shaman will need to journey to his spirit guides for advice on the cause of the illness and the best means of its cure. For many shamans, soul parts are lost as a result of three possible causes:

I. Through the Actions of the Client Herself

Perhaps the client senses that she has behaved unethically or dishonourably towards another person and carries the weight of that 'sin' on her soul. (For a more in-depth discussion of this see my book *The Sin Eater's Last Confessions*). The first step of many shamans is to elicit a 'confession' (in modern terms this amounts to simply letting her talk about it and responding without judgement, in a similar way to that used by the Western psychotherapeutic schools who offer a 'talking cure'). The pain of the soul is eased by confession and knowing that it will no longer be subjected to the distress caused by guilt the soul may return on its own.

Knowing the 'sins' of his patient the shaman may also intervene on her behalf in order to make amends – for example by making a journey to the power animals or guardian spirits of the person sinned against to ask forgiveness. This may be enough to break the spell or these spirits may ask the shaman's client to atone for her wrongdoings in a more formal way, always with her interests at heart and a desire to serve the common good.

Such demands are often practical in nature. The person may be told to return something she has stolen or to reconcile a feud, for example. If this is done, then again, the pain of the soul is eased.

At the same time, we may sometimes carry guilt or shame for things we believe we are guilty of when these things were not actually our fault. We may carry the shame of a failed marriage, for example, even though both parties were to blame. Often people who have been abused can also carry shame, assuming at an unconscious level that they must somehow have encouraged or caused the abuse. Confession in such cases should not be made lightly and it is important for the client to understand the real situation and circumstances because accepting the blame for everything is itself a form of power loss.

2. Through the Actions of Others

The experiences of a soul lost through abuse are ones of pain and fear. In these circumstances the shaman will begin by re-empowering his client in the way previously described (e.g. energy realignment and power animal retrieval) in order to strengthen her energy body and spirit. If he does not do so the soul he returns for her later may simply leak away once more from an energy body so wounded that it is shredded and full of holes.

The healer will next journey to meet the missing soul in the middle world. He knows that the soul will not have wandered far from the physical community and he also understands the affinity of human souls for trees and water and this is where he will begin his search. Other places to look are those where the trauma first took place (for example the childhood home or the scene of an accident). Your spirits will guide you in this.

When he finds this missing soul part the shaman must deal with it kindly since it may be fearful, tearful or confused. The shaman must therefore be sensitive, gentle, understanding – and firm. *Parental* in a word. Explaining what has happened to the missing soul, he will tell it that its owner is longing for its return and is now more powerful and able to resist the attacks from others that caused the soul pain in the past. He will ask the soul part to return with him.

Sometimes it is willing to do so, sometimes not. If it is, the shaman will gather it in his arms and carry it back to his patient where he will blow it back into her energy body in the same way as in a power retrieval.

If it will not return willingly the shaman will ask what the soul part needs in order to feel protected and cared for so it is prepared to come back. He may then need to go back to his client and advise her of the necessary life changes she must make in order for the soul to return. The client may have to enact these changes before the soul retrieval can continue but sometimes a promise to do so is enough to reassure the lost soul and once the shaman relays this commitment to it the soul will return with him.

3. Through Shock

Sometimes we can be so scared or traumatised by an event that we literally 'jump out of our skins'. Haitian shamans have a word for this. They call it *seiziman*. In Peru it is called *manchare* and it is believed to be more common in children because their souls are not so fixed in the body, although it can affect adults too.

It is a state of such severe shock to the system that it causes physical or emotional pain. It is the agony of a wife who is told that her husband is dead, the hurt and disbelief we feel when we discover that our partner has been unfaithful or is leaving us, the spaced-out stunned sensation that follows a fright or a physical accident.

In all of these circumstances the soul leaves the body in temporary shock. Often it does not leave completely but steps outside of our skin until the physical body recovers. When we are able to gather our senses again we automatically begin to draw our spirit back in. Sometimes, however, we need a little help with this before we can re-energise ourselves and get on with our lives.

From his consultation with his client and his spirits, the shaman will know if the soul loss is a temporary state of affairs where the soul is still attached to the body and is simply taking its time to find a way back. He may also be able to see the disembodied soul through the power of his gazing and it may appear like a luminous shadow of the physical self attached to the body via a cord of energy.

Cases like this are less extreme forms of soul loss and therefore demand less extreme forms of healing, although there is still some urgency for the healing to take place as the cord that holds the soul to the body can be broken or eroded over time and the spirit can then drift away and become more fully lost. The shaman's job is to help the soul ease itself back into the physical body.

This is accomplished, typically, by making the client's physical body the most attractive and comfortable place for the soul to be. In cases of seiziman in Haiti the client may be massaged, for example, treated to a healing bath with lots of sweet-smelling flowers and herbs or a short ceremony may be performed for her during which she will be reassured that she is loved and admired by the community who want her back.

Translated into Western healing methods this may also equate to giving our client a massage with sweet-smelling oils, allowing her to talk through her problems, giving her reiki or reflexology, praying for her, and so on, all of it designed to relax and empower her so the soul feels comforted and welcomed home.

In Peru a ritual may be performed where the shaman accompanies the client to the place where the accident occurred or the trauma or shock took place and negotiates with the spirit of that place (see chapter seven) to release the parts of the client that it is holding on to, leaving flowers and incense in exchange for letting the soul return.

He will then instruct the client to breathe back in the power that she feels was lost there.

This is another practice which has now been adopted by Western psychotherapists and counsellors. Some also take their clients to the physical location where power was lost and there is a growing trend for reconciliation meetings between the perpetrators and victims of crimes; the point being that when we are shocked or suffer a trauma of this kind we can often make it a bigger event in our minds than it actually was. When we see it for what it is, however, it is rarely as big as we thought and, realising this, we take our power back from it.

The shaman will recognise that the soul is home by the return of colour to his client's cheeks, by her lighter step and by what she says. If he is at all concerned that the soul has not returned he may undertake one of the other healings described above and, particularly, may journey into the Otherworld to escort the lost soul home with him. This may not always be necessary in cases of shock where deliberate abuse is not the cause but the shaman's spirits will advise him of this.

Exploration

Find three different clients you can work with to explore these methods practically. Again, in normal circumstances, I would not recommend that you work with friends or family but you can do so for the purposes of practice. *Be extremely careful as you take these first exploratory steps and very sensitive in respect of what you say and do.* Ideally your client should only experience, from their perspective, a positive and uplifting chat (in the case of confession), a restful lie-down while you massage or minister to them (in the case of a soul lost through shock) or a time of relaxation with eyes closed in the case of a soul retrieval where you are required to locate and rescue a soul lost through trauma. If your client asks what you did for them it is better to give as little information as possible to avoid re-awakening old feelings and memories. You can simply say that you returned good energy to their souls.

Summary: A Framework for Healing

A useful framework for shamanic soul healing is as follows. Don't take this as a rule for every case; use your own creativity as well. But it is perhaps wise to stick to these steps until you are fully confident with all the techniques.

- Create a sacred environment then call for power from your spirit allies who will assist the healing work. *This is always the most important first step.*

- Examine your client's energy body. If necessary (and it usually is) work on this first to ensure that it is properly aligned for the return of power.

- Remove unhealthy energies. If any extraction work is needed do this before power or soul retrieval to create a safe, clean, space that delicate energies can return to.

- Return power. Power retrieval is often required before soul retrieval. Sometimes full soul retrieval is not necessary and power only needs to be returned. Power retrieval also gives the client the energy she needs to anchor the soul parts you will return to her later.

- Return the missing soul. If soul retrieval is indicated, from your discussions with your client and your consultations with spirit, decide if the soul parts have been lost through guilt she is carrying for actions she is ashamed of. If so help her to talk through these actions ('confess'), then journey to your spirit advisors to find a way that she can make amends for her behaviour. *When you present this information to her make sure you do so in a non-judgemental way so you do not reinforce any guilt she already feels.*

- If she is carrying guilt that does not rightfully belong to her because it actually stems from the actions of others (e.g. in the case of sexual abuse), help your client to see the truth of this and then perform a power or soul retrieval for her.

- If the soul parts have been lost through trauma due to the actions of others, journey to your spirit allies and ask for their assistance to locate the missing parts. Begin your search at the moment and in the place that you sense the damage was done – the town, street, house she lived in when the abuse took place; the age she was at the time or the year and month when the incident happened, for example. This is the moment at which the soul was lost. If you do not find the soul part there look around you for trees and water.

- When you find the lost soul explain to it what has happened and encourage it to return with you. When it is ready to do so, gather this energy in your arms and, coming back from your journey, blow this soul fragment into the energy body of your client just as you did in the power retrieval exercise, then rattle around her to seal in the energy.

- If the soul is lost through seiziman or manchare – intense short-term shock or fear – the energy of your client may not be far away and the best way to recover it is to comfort and relax your client so that the soul finds it desirable to return. Singing gently to her as you offer her a relaxing massage, like a lullaby to a child, is a very simple, beautiful ceremony. The soul finds this comforting and will follow the song back home.

- When the healing is complete offer thanks to your spirits and close the sacred space.

Healing Yourself

To use these techniques of healing on others you need to know how they feel. We cannot heal someone else unless we know how the healing works from both sides and unless we feel as whole as we can be in ourselves. This of course is a life-long journey. While we are alive we are always trying to complete ourselves so there is no 'right time' to begin as a shamanic healer, only when we and our spirits believe we are ready. We cannot fix *everything* in ourselves either before we start to heal others because just when we think we have it all sorted we may find ourselves in a different situation which causes us pain or problems. Self-knowledge is important, however, as well as an ongoing desire to heal, to learn from our dis-eases and to be as whole as we can be at this point in our lives, knowing that we can always get better and that, indeed, this is our intention.

Ideally at this part of your training then (especially if you have never had soul retrieval or shamanic healing before) you will book an appointment for yourself with a reputable healer so you can experience what it feels like to be healed in this way. The following exercises will also give you a sense of healing.

It is not just 'clients' who carry pain; we all do (we are all the 'clients' of spirit). Every one of us has been wounded at some point whether this was an emotional hurt, a physical trauma, mental anguish or stress, we have all felt it. A good healer is not a 'perfect sorted being'; to be effective we need to know and have experienced such wounds or we cannot identify and empathise with the experience of our clients.

At the same time we must also have passed through or come to terms with this pain and found an answer to it that at some level works for us so we are as balanced as we can be and can also lead others to wholeness. As Eliade writes, the shaman is 'a sick man who has been cured, who has succeeded in curing himself' (or at least begun the process). Once he has achieved this he is able to help others because he knows 'the mechanism, or rather, the theory of illness'.

Such knowledge requires mindfulness. Even when he is suffering the healer will be learning from his pain so he under-stands how it manifests, the course it takes through his body, the way it feels at each stage and how it can be healed.

Illness is a 'theory' because, in a sense, it does not exist. It is our reaction to an event, our attachment to it or our affinity for the energy it creates in us that actually causes dis-ease, not the event itself. An illness is only an illness if we allow it to be and agree that it has more power than we do. There are many examples of people who have overcome debilitating diseases or even avoided death because they believed otherwise.

Confession

Confession enables you to acknowledge the wrongs you have done (or believe you have done) to others, to express remorse and to remove this unhelpful energy from your body. It is, in a sense, another form of spirit extraction. Holding on to shame and the energy it creates will lead to illness as we punish ourselves 'internally' for the guilt we feel. Speaking it out and externalising our pain allows the energy body to realign itself so we can be healthy again.

We do not always have a healer or even a friend we can confess to but this is less important because we – and our spirits – can be our own witnesses and, knowing the scale of our 'crime', we also know the penance we must serve to be well.

This confession ritual comes from the Welsh sin eating tradition but is known in other cultures too. It is easy to perform. All you need is a length of string, approximately twelve to eighteen inches in length, and a fireproof container.

Take the string in your hands and begin to speak aloud your 'sins' against others or against yourself if you feel you have also let yourself down in the past somehow. As you name each sin make a knot in the string and before you draw it tight focus on getting out all the negative energies associated with that event. Cry or scream if you want to – this is between you and the spirits (who already know what you have done); no-one else can see you – so you can be as honest in words and emotions as you need to be. Offer your sins to the spirits so they may transmute their energy and use it in positive work for others. *Learn* from the sin as well so you discover more about yourself, the situations or relationships in which the behaviour you exhibited is likely to arise; you can then make your patterns conscious and, through this, avoid them in future. Then bind each of your sins into the string by pulling the knot tight.

Do this three times, even if there are more things you wish to confess – you can always repeat this ritual at another time – then place the string in the container and set fire to it. Watch as it burns and see the energy of your actions being returned to the universe where it can do some good for others.

Be aware during this time of any thoughts or feelings that come to you about how you might make amends to the person you have hurt by your previous actions. If you possibly can, do what is asked of you to make things right, *but do nothing that might cause further harm to another person or to yourself.*

Retrieving the Soul through Warriorship
We have all experienced shock and pain as a result of the behaviour of others towards us. In those moments, shamans say that part of our soul is lost and takes flight from the body to escape further harm. We must retrieve these soul fragments in order to be whole.

Think back to an event in your life when you know that damage was done to your soul. You may have experienced this as an empty pain in your solar plexus, as a feeling of disconnection and weakness or a sensation of not being fully present some time after or during the event itself. It was at this moment that the soul part was lost.

Perhaps this took place many years ago, perhaps it was only yesterday. Whenever it was, a younger you suffered; the you now is older, wiser, more resourceful and more powerful. You are stronger than the soul part that left and more able to be your own warrior in facing the challenges your younger self could not.

Journey in the usual way into the middle world with the intention of finding that part of yourself that was lost through earlier trauma. Remember the shaman's technique of looking first in the community. In your case this will be the location you were at or the place you were living when the incident took place. If you do not find the soul part immediately make a spiral out from this place, looking for trees and water as you search the whole environment.

When you find the missing soul it will normally have the appearance of a younger you, at the age you were when this energy was lost. If it looks even younger than you remember this is likely to be because the event you have in mind actually stems from an earlier incident when the energetic pattern was set up that eventually led to your hurt. If it looks older than you expect, it is because the event itself was not the moment when the soul left; it was actually lost later when the effects of this incident were felt by your energy body.

Whatever the age of the soul part and however it appears to you, this is the part to work with, the energy you most need to recover at this time and which you will be returning using the technique that follows.

Approach the lost soul and talk to it. Explain what has happened to it, tell it you love it and want it to return with you but there are a number of trials you must face together first. If you can complete these tasks the pain of the past will be released as the energy surrounding it is diffused and you will be able to return together.

The first of these challenges is to cross the quaking Earth. See before you a narrow path that crosses a deep swamp on either side. If you fall into this swamp you will be sucked under. The ground around and in front of you is shaking as if in an earth-quake, making the crossing more difficult, but you must cross it together if the soul is to be returned. You have a choice of whether to accept this challenge or turn away. If you accept you must help the soul to cross, following behind as its guardian.

Your second challenge is to pass through the flaming forest.

All around you trees are crashing to the ground as a forest fire rages out of control, destroying all in front of it. The heat is searing and the flames singe your hair and face but you will survive and pass through it safely as long as you both stay on the same narrow path. You must focus and not be distracted by falling trees or tongues of flame in order to keep to the path. Lead the soul part safely through to the other side.

Your third challenge is to cross the frozen sea. A vast ocean stands before you. The water is ice cold and giant icebergs crash together in the deep waves beyond the shore. Far away in the distance is a tiny island, your destination, but in order to get there you must avoid the icebergs and survive the icy waters. You know you can only do this if you stick to the narrow channel that passes between these giant blocks of ice. Your task is to lead the soul part safely through these treacherous seas to the island ahead of you.

Your fourth challenge awaits on this island. As you land a great whirlwind sweeps towards you, lifting all in its path. Your first instinct is to run but something within you knows that the only way to survive is to stay calm and relax. If you resist the wind will crush you; if you relax you will be able to bend with it so you remain unharmed. Stay calm and allow the wind to lift you both and take you where it will.

Finally, you are set gently back to Earth. What faces you now is your fifth and final challenge. You are back in the situation that caused the original trauma. This is the event that your soul part left to escape. As tired as you both are, you are warriors. Soul parts may leave for many reasons – the physical pain of a beating, the emotional pain of divorce or an act of betrayal by a lover, the mental anguish caused by continual pressures, the spiritual pain of a loss of faith. Whatever the reason in your case the event must be dealt with.

Your role is to act as guardian and protector of the lost soul but it is the soul itself that must deal with this situation. With you as an ally it must go back to this original scene and, using your combined strengths, do battle with and defeat the perpetrator of this disempowering event. Offer your support and assistance from the empowered perspective of someone older, wiser and more resourceful who has already lived through this event and survived to become more powerful as a consequence. You can also call upon your allies to intervene on your behalf. They are your resources now – and they cannot be defeated by a human enemy, no matter how strong.

When the battle is over, return with the soul part the way you have come and, as you stand once again before the quaking Earth, embrace each other. You have been through a mythical challenge and an adventure together and are now inseparably one once again. Return to ordinary reality when you are ready, knowing that you now have this power back.

This process is interesting from both a spiritual and a psychological perspective. Notice that all of the elements play a role in your journey – Earth, Fire, Water and Air (the wind that lifts you). As you pass through each of these you receive the healing gifts they offer. You are grounded by the Earth, purified by Fire, washed clean by the Water and lifted by the Air. You are strengthened by these forces with every step you take along the path to your final challenge.

Psychologically, you are also reintegrating the lost soul at every step since you actually work together to bring the soul part home. You are able to use the inner resources of the older you who can look at the hurtful events of the past with a sense of detachment and objectivity so you see it for what it really was rather than the terrifying catastrophe such events may seem to a younger self.

In helping your younger self you also learn compassion, understanding and love for yourself, as you were then and as you are now, which many people who have been hurt or abused find difficult.

For these reasons this is a very powerful method of soul healing. My workshop participants, some of whom have years of experience as healers, often find it the most powerful healing they have undertaken. Be gentle on yourself for the next few days after this healing therefore and allow yourself some time before attempting the other exercises in this chapter or moving on to the next one.

Quick Test 5

1. What is spirit extraction and how do you perform one?
2. What is power retrieval and how is it performed?
3. List three reasons that soul parts might leave and one thing in each case you might do to get them back
4. Write out from memory the checklist or framework for a typical shamanic healing

Exercises

Continue to practice your journeying and dream journal work. Before you go on to the next chapter, please also undertake these pieces of self-reflection.

Confession

What did the exercise on confession teach you? Did you feel any change in your physical or energy body during or after this work?

The Warrior Journey (Power Return)

What did this exercise teach you? Do you sense any change/s now this journey has been made?

Spiritual Advice

Once you have completed the warrior journey exercise make a journey to your tutelary spirit (upper world) and ask for advice or information on what to do next. Are there any practical actions you should take or any things to avoid to ensure that you do not lose spiritual energy or soul parts in future? What forms of protection are suggested? What physical actions might you take in order to anchor the returned energy in your body?

Six

Counselling and the Future

In this Chapter

Shamanic counselling, shamanic core process, divination: rock divination, journeying for guidance to a future self, lucid dreaming, the vision quest and the night vigil.

Reading for this Chapter

Welcome Home, Sandra Ingerman (a basic introduction to soul retrieval written from a Western 'core shamanic' perspective. The process described is very simplified and unlike actual – field – shamanic techniques but is of use when working with Western clients).

Equipment Required

Drum
Drumming tape
Tape recorder
A rock, approximately the size of a grapefruit with at least four sides to it

Life After Soul Retrieval

When soul parts or power are returned to a client or negative energies removed – indeed, when any form of energetic work is done – it can take a little while for these energies to be reintegrated into the client's system because her spiritual or energetic make-up has been changed and she needs to get used to this.

To assist this process our spirit allies sometimes offer advice or counsel through us to a client as the healing is taking place, or on subsequent journeys. This is often practical in nature and may be suggestions about herbs the client can work with (see chapter eight) in order to further restore her power or some daily exercise or discipline the client might try (meditation, or even something as everyday and simple as gardening or dancing) in order to ground her energy and bring it back into the body. When this happens the shaman is beginning to move somewhat out of the role of healer and more into diviner or oracle for the client's future and her counsellor or life coach on how best to 'be' in the world.

Sometimes, also, a client will come to a shaman with questions about her life or choices she needs to make. What she requires from the practitioner then is not so much healing but guidance. There are various ways that the shaman might help with this. In this chapter we look at methods of shamanic counselling and divination that can provide the insights she needs.

Shamanic Counselling

Shamanic counselling is a modern adaptation of traditional journeying techniques. It is a process whereby the client informs the shaman of the question or need for information that she has. The shaman will then express this as a positive intention and journey to his spirit allies who provide the answers required.

The main point of difference to a normal journey is that for the benefit of the client the shaman will usually speak out loud the visions that he sees and the information he receives. He may, for example, describe the terrain he is travelling in on the journey, the animals or allies he encounters – what they look like, who they are, what they say and do, etc. All of this will have spiritual or symbolic resonance for the client which may be unknown to the shaman. His job, only, is to report accurately what he sees and senses.

Some modern shamans also record the journey they are taking as it unfolds so the client has a record she can refer to.

Because of his need to speak out loud it is usual for the modern shaman to wear headphones and to listen to a drumming tape instead of drumming for himself as he journeys since the drum would make it difficult for information to be clearly recorded or for the client to hear it spoken.

When the journey ends the shaman returns to consciousness and may, if he and the client both wish, listen to the tape he has made. This often prompts other observations, insights and memories from the journey and allows the information to be filled out for the client who may choose to take notes. The shaman and client then discuss the information and arrive together at an answer to the client's original question.

Shamanic Core Process

Another means of shamanic counselling is to instruct the client in how to journey for herself and guide her to find her own answers. A technique that can help this is shamanic core process, a modern approach that combines shamanism with the 'psychological processing' of psychoanalysis (a form of therapy that is sometimes less threatening to some clients who would rather not hear about 'spirits' and 'lost souls').

The shaman guides a journey taken by the client, using drum and voice to gently direct her through the stages of entry to the lower world to meet her own spirit allies (see chapter one). Again, if the client is new to shamanic work these allies can be described instead as 'aspects of the self' – i.e. the different powers we hold within ourselves. Putting it in these more familiar psychological terms means the client may be able to engage more fully with the process.

It is also important to remember that for people not used to shamanic work there can still be a fear of the 'lower world' as being a scary or even demonised place. They may see it in Christian terms, as the opposite of 'Heaven' (i.e. 'Hell') and be unnerved by it. It is therefore important to put the lower world in context, as a place where specific types of information (or arche-types) can be found and with none of the negative judgements that Christianity has imposed on it. Sometimes it is simply best to say that you are helping the client to take a guided visualisation deeper into herself.

In a way this is 'shamanic trickery' but more importantly it is a means to effective healing through the practitioner's agreement to simply use another form or words which corresponds to the client's model of understanding. The outcome of the healing work is the same however, whatever words are used.

From the perspective of the shaman the client is guided to meet her personal spiritual teacher in whatever form is most acceptable to her, who will pass on insights and information about that person which only they could know and which are helpful in understanding the bigger picture and patterns of her life. This teacher will also take the role of a guardian and protector, leading the client to recover her power or find answers to her questions.

For clarity the journey should be guided in stages with the shaman drumming at times and speaking at others while the drum is played more softly. A typical 'script' for this journey might be as follows:

Lie down on your back and make yourself comfortable. Close your eyes, relax and take a few deep breaths. Good. I am going to be playing the drum while we take this visualisation. This is simply to help you relax. As you follow its sound you'll find that you can let go of tensions and gain information more clearly. This information may come in images, in words or in feelings.

Now firstly, I would like you to see in your mind's eye a place you know (in ordinary reality) that might take you down into the Earth in some way – such as a cave or the roots of a tree – and therefore, symbolically, deeper into yourself. Raise your hand when you see this place clearly and then we will move on to the next part.

Drum as she looks for this place until she raises her hand.

Now you are in a threshold place, a place which is deeper than ordinary reality and where everything has meaning. Look for a source of light and walk towards that. Let me know when you see it.

Drum as she looks for the light until she raises her hand.

Now walk into the light and as you do so you will find that it becomes another world with its own landscape. Step into it and look around you. Find, if you can, running water like a stream or a river and follow it so you trace it back to its source. Let me know when you are there.

Drum as she proceeds until she raises her hand.

Now look around you and you will see an ally of some kind – perhaps in the form of an animal which has the special qualities you need. Or it could be in another form, such as a guide, an object of power or a kind and enlightened being. However it appears it is also an aspect of your power, qualities you have that can help you. You will see this animal or guide four times in all, perhaps in different positions or from different perspectives. Let me know when you have done this.

Drum as she proceeds, until she raises her hand.

Speak with this ally, this aspect of yourself, and ask any questions you would like answers to, knowing that this ally knows your true thoughts and feelings better than anyone else in the world. Raise your hand when you have all the information you need.

Drum as she proceeds until she raises her hand.

[This is an optional stage which can be taken if power retrieval is necessary in addition to counselling]: *Now reach out your hands and draw this ally to you so its power and energy merge with yours. This will give you greater strength, clarity and power in your life and you will always be able to access this ally in future so you can draw from its wisdom and guidance. In other words you will have that greater sense of love and knowledge always within you. Let me know when you feel you have made this strong connection to your ally.*

Drum as she proceeds until she raises her hand.

Now retrace your steps back from this landscape, through your cave or other means you took to enter this world and come back to the room where you lay. Bring your attention back to your body and your awareness back to this reality and to me, keeping your eyes closed. Let me know when you feel yourself back.

Drum as she makes her ascent to normal consciousness until she raises her hand.

Good. Now I'm just going to drum a bit more quickly to 'wake us up' and get our energies flowing again.

Drum using a 'callback signal' – a more rapid drumming rhythm – for 30 seconds or so.

Good. Now take a few deep breaths and, when you are ready, open your eyes.

It is a good idea now to offer your client a glass of cool mineral water to bring her round further. Then discuss with her the information (and the power) she has retrieved.

Divination

Divination takes many forms, even in our own Celtic past. Casting lots was the expertise of one Germanic tribe. There is also a system that came from Irish travellers which uses divination by bird flight. In Scottish sources there is divination by reading the formations of clouds or the smoke from an open fire. In all cases two things are necessary:

- Faith in omens, synchronicities, the coming together of forces in Nature as the visible face of spirit and in our spirit allies to talk to us through symbols and intermediary forms such as cloud shapes or the patterns of birds in flight
- The ability of the shaman to walk between worlds and enter the betwixt and between place at the threshold of ordinary and non-ordinary reality so that everyday things are perceived in an uncommon way. When this is achieved anything we see can, with intent, be a message from the spiritual world

There is a story from Wales for example (told in my book *The Sin Eater's Last Confessions*) of a man who visits a diviner with a question and is told to come back on Wednesday at noon. The diviner does nothing until dawn on the appointed day. Then he gets out of bed and puts on his trousers but not his shirt and one sock but not both. He goes to the doorway of his house and stands on the threshold, neither in nor out, then closes his eyes.

He turns three times, opening his eyes briefly at each turn, and taking in the things he sees – a tree, a cloud, a bird, for example. Then he creates in his mind a story that involves all three which in some way relates to his client's question.

In all cases the diviner is in the betwixt and between place – he awakes at dawn (not day or night), he *half*-dresses, he stands in the doorway (neither out nor in) and he both closes and opens his eyes. His client is told to return at noon for the answer, which is neither morning nor afternoon, and on Wednesday, the middle of the week. Through these actions the diviner is in communion with the spirits of Nature and receives his information from them by always remaining in the threshold.

Exploration: The Threshold Place

Being on the threshold and taking counsel from the natural world is one approach of divination. To assess it for yourself, first hold your question in mind and then find three places that represent thresholds or boundaries of some kind – the spot where curb meets road, the shadow of a tree ends, or the gateway to a garden for example.

In each place close your eyes and turn three times, then open them and make a mental note of the first thing you see. When this is done write all three things down and create a story from them. In some way that you will recognise this story is the answer to your question. Does the answer you have make sense?

Rock Divination

The technique above is somewhat similar to this one – an approach used by the Sioux Indians – in the sense that it places the shaman outside of ordinary reality and puts his faith in the immaterial world to bring him the answers he needs. Here the shaman, in a walk of attention (see chapter three), will allow himself to be drawn to a particular rock, the spirit of which calls to him in answer to a question he holds in mind.

He will sit with this rock, gazing it (see chapter three) and taking his consciousness into it, examining it from at least four sides. He may see a star on one side, an animal on another, and so on, and will make a note of each of these representations of spirit. Finally he will be left with four pieces of information. Once again he will then dream himself into these until he can find a composite story that answers his question. These are the facts he will act upon.

Exploration: The Voice of the Rock

Follow the Sioux approach, allowing yourself to be called to a rock that attracts you and then gaze it from four sides. Make a note of the things that speak to you. Then use your imagination and creativity to generate a story that includes them all and which has a relationship to your question. Does this answer make sense?

Journeying for Guidance to a Future Self

To the shaman the concepts of time and space are meaningless. In his journeys he voyages beyond both so it is quite possible for him to enter a potential future for himself or a client and to meet with the person he or his client may choose to become and thereby see directly the consequences of an action he may take. This is another form of divination.

Technically, this is a middle world journey since the shaman is effectively moving forward in time to see himself or his client in some future situation that results because of a decision he or that client may make.

The journey is taken in the normal way (see chapter one) with your client's question to guide your intention. As always, call first for your spirit helpers and then ask to be shown the future that results from the decision your client might make.

If your client has a question such as 'Should I do X or Y?' (e.g. move to a new town or stay where I am?) ask first to meet with the future spirit or essence of the client who *does* move then enter into conversation with that future self. Notice as well how the future feels and looks. What is its mood? Is your client happy and fulfilled? Is your client with other people who seem meaningful to her (and in what ways?) When you have the answers you need thank the future client for her guidance and then ask your spirits to take you to the client who does *not* move and do the same.

When you are ready to return, retrace your steps back from the Otherworld and bring your consciousness to everyday reality. You can now tell your client what you have seen and suggest a best course of action based on the information you have.

It is also possible to undertake this journey and to speak it aloud at each stage in the way of shamanic counselling so the client shares the experience with you.

Lucid Dreaming

Lucid dreaming is another form of spiritual consultation which facilitates out-of-body experiences, spirit guidance and practical journeying during sleep. The method takes a little practice but is achievable since the same energy fields are involved, the human and the transpersonal, enabling you to connect with another or to visit a distant location without needing to do so physically, by guiding the energy body to separate from you during the act of dreaming and then directing its actions with the power of intention.

An American shaman tells the story of her experiments in

lucid dreaming when she was first learning the technique. She and a friend some States away arranged to dream together on a specific night every week and to share adventures this way, and then to phone each other the next day to see if they had common experiences during sleep.

Their procedure was to ensure that they were both in bed asleep at a specified time and to intend that, whatever their dreaming adventures, they would be joined in them by the other. Both would start out in the dream at a specific and pre-determined landmark known to them both in ordinary reality by holding the image of this place in mind as they began to drift into sleep. Any commonalities of dreaming experience they reported the next day were verification of contact during sleep.

One night, having gone to bed and begun to dream at the appointed time, the shaman was surprised to see her friend driving along a particular American highway since this was nothing like the dreaming destination they normally started from. Even stranger was the fact that the highway was interspersed with images of a tropical beach scene. When she awoke the shaman dismissed the experience as too jumbled and unlikely to have been a real lucid dream: her friend would have been asleep in bed not driving and the beach scene in any case seemed nonsense.

When she spoke to her friend next day, however, she reported that she had been late home from work that night so had not been able to take part in the dreaming exercise. Instead she had been driving home – on the exact highway the shaman had seen – and, realising she was late for the dreaming experiment had focused on the only thing she had to hand at the time in order to transmit images of that – which happened to be a postcard featuring a Caribbean beach that was on her passenger seat. The dream had been accurate despite its seeming confusion.

How can we use dreaming like this in a practical way? Well, we might use it to check on loved ones to ensure that they are safe, to visit libraries to learn new skills, for research or for advice on healing and empowerment through dreaming consultations with great healers and spiritual leaders in this world or the next. We can, of course, also use it for seeing the future.

One of my students, through lucid dreaming, was able to predict a difficult situation he would find himself in on a trip to a foreign country, 1,000 miles from his home and a month or so after the dream itself. This student did not listen to his dream, however, and made his journey anyway – with the exact consequences he had foreseen. In circumstances like this, with advance knowledge, it is possible to avoid some situations altogether and ensure that the events we have seen never take place. That, however, is a matter of choice!

Exploration 1: Solo Practice

To begin dreaming in this way, lie comfortably in bed as normal and, just as you feel yourself slipping into the meditative state between wakefulness and sleep, send a precise and deliberate command to yourself that tonight you will dream and be aware you are dreaming and in control of your actions throughout.

When you recognise during sleep that you are in a dream you must then separate yourself from the dreamer so you can control your actions. The simplest way to do so is to pull back your energy from the character you are in the dream and position yourself a few feet behind and slightly above this person. You are then able to see as they see and to guide their interactions with others.

If you would like information on your future or are dreaming on behalf of a friend or client, intend that you and/or they are part of a scene and, through the dream, gather information on the situation they are in, just as if you were journeying.

Exploration 2: The Art of Dreaming

Arrange with a friend to set up a dreaming experiment. Agree that you will both go to bed at a pre-determined time and meet at a certain place in the dreamscape with the intention – both of you – of exploring the future outcome of a choice that has to be made by her or you.

Notice the interactions between the two of you and what is said and done as well as the environment around you and the landscape you are in. Are there any distinguishing landmarks, signs or symbols you can use later to confirm your experiences? In answer to your intention, what was the choice that you or she made and what does the future look like as an outcome of this?

Next day meet with your friend and discuss your separate dream experiences. What do they have in common? Did your friend see the same things as you? What did you speak of in the dream – can you both remember the content? Do you share a sense of the future and of the choice that needs to be made?

The Vision Quest

Sometimes we need more than insight into the repercussions of a particular choice and more than a general sense of a future. We need a vision for that future.

The vision quest is a deeper and more profound act of divination in the sense that it can provide us with guidance for our entire lives, give us greater awareness and clarity around our purpose and enable us to change who we are or have become if that is our choice.

The quest is a spiritual phenomenon known in all traditions of the world, including the Native American with which it is most associated but also Buddhism, Hinduism, the 'walkabout' of the Australian Aborigine and shamanism in all its forms. It is a way of getting back to basics so we can work more effectively and pro-actively with the energetic world around us.

The fundamental principle behind the quest is that we all need to spend time alone where we can focus on defining our relationship to the world and how we will live in it; for looking within ourselves, for making commitments to a particular spiritual and philosophical approach to the world and for challenging that view by testing ourselves so that when this period of aloneness ends we can affirm, stand up for and defend our personal beliefs.

Among the Dagara of Africa for example a young man is expected to go out into the wilderness alone and then to be instructed by his Elders in the ways of spirit. Among the Shuar of the Amazon there are monsters that must be defeated before the person who quests can return to the tribe a man and the initiate must go into the jungle alone in order to find them. In Haiti initiation takes the form of a prescribed course of isolation and trials undertaken before the whole community. All include an element of time spent alone so the individual can find his spiritual power.

There is a Lakota prayer for the vision quest, a personal prayer for every seeker, which goes:

Great Spirit, whose voice I hear in the winds,
And whose breath gives life to all the world...
Make me wise so I may understand the things you have taught my
*   people,*
Let me learn the lessons you have hidden in every leaf and rock;
I seek strength, not to be greater than my brother
But to fight my greatest enemy – myself...
So when life fades as the fading sunset,
My spirit may come to you without shame

This is the point of the vision quest: that there are lessons 'hidden in every leaf and rock' and that Nature will communicate with us through these symbols and signs if we remain still long enough to sense them. Then we can meet our maker without shame, having been guided by our visions to do the right things in our lives.

The anthropologist Arnold van Gennep described the characteristics of all rites of passage as a severance from normal habitual practices; a time of aloneness at the 'threshold' of personal change where we journey deep into ourselves, see what we have created, and take steps to renew ourselves; and finally an emergence back into the community with a clearer way of seeing our lives and typically with tasks to be performed so that we may change and, through this, change the world around us for the good.

In traditional societies this three-stage process is normally represented by a period of fasting and prayer in preparation for the quest, during which the candidate readies himself for separation from the normal, expected and habitual life of his people. In certain communities, most prominently those in North America, this may be followed by a sweatlodge where the group will purify and cleanse itself to remove all traces of the old.

After the sweat the candidate will enter the threshold stage, walking alone into the natural landscape where he will remain in isolation from others for a period of several days. He will draw on his intuition and inspiration to find the place most conducive to spiritual experience. Sometimes this will be an active search for a particular power spot but often it is a sensation of being drawn to the right area and a feeling of peace when he finds it.

He will then create a sacred circle on the ground, of rocks and other natural materials, and this circle will become his home for the period of his quest. He must not move from this place but remain in stillness, journeying within himself for answers and watching his environment for clues.

There must be no distractions, no making notes or keeping diaries or marking off the days – all the typical distractions of our overly-analytical society – instead the candidate must remain focused and intent.

The four sacred questions the seeker takes with him and which he must answer *honestly and fearlessly* – no matter where they lead him – at this time are:

Where have I come from?

What forces and people have influenced my life and made me who I am?

Who am I now?

What have I become as a result of these influences?

Where am I going?

How would I like to change and what should my direction be now?

Who will come with me?

Which of the people in my life are good for me and aid the flowering of my soul and which of them hold me back in my spiritual quest? And what changes am I prepared to make in this respect?

They are good questions to ask and if we answer them truthfully they will teach us all we need to know about ourselves and our lives and the purpose of our souls.

For modern vision questers this requirement to sit still, to remain quiet and not distract oneself with trivia is one of the most demanding – and most powerful – aspects of the experience. It will typically produce an initial feeling of boredom, irritation, sometimes frustration, even despondency, because it is so alien to our way of life. After a while, however, you will notice that you are slowing down to the natural pace of the Earth, that *its* rhythms have become *your* rhythms and that a dialogue can now begin between you. The features of the landscape and the natural world become in themselves the answers to your deepest questions of existential meaning.

Andy, a computer programmer, tells how he had been so bored during the first day of his quest and felt so alone and frightened at night as the forest came alive with shadows and sounds that he had spent his second day in tears.

Then something magical began to happen. I found that layers of me began to drop away – and that the environment itself became a part of me and started responding to my questions. I would be thinking for example of the break-up of my marriage and all the things my ex-wife had done to hurt me. Then I would realise that she hadn't actually done anything to me. She had behaved in a certain way, which was simply a reflection of how she led her life, and I had responded in another way, the way I lead mine. Any pain I felt between those two ways of acting was not in the behaviour itself but in my sense of it. No harm had been done to me; I had done it to myself.

And then I began to see the pattern of my responses going back through all my relationships, right back to the time when as a child, I decided it was better to be defensive, to attack first and to subtly destroy my relationships because I knew that was less painful than having people leave me as my mother had. She had left me, it was true. But she hadn't destroyed every other relationship in my life. I had done that myself by deciding to attack first so I couldn't go on blaming her either.

And then I thought how everything could have been so different if I had made other decisions – until eventually I got so frustrated at myself and my own mistakes that I started to cry. I was surprised at myself; I hadn't cried for years. But it felt good. And then – at that exact moment – it started to rain, absolutely pour down. It was like the world around me was crying too.

I was drenched, miserable, cursing and swearing at myself and the world. And the world did the same right back, blowing up a gale which drove the rain into my face. And then I started to laugh at myself. Here I was again, dwelling on the past, beating myself up, blaming myself for everything, destroying my relationship with myself this time. It was the same pattern! I decided that the only way I could go was forward and to start from scratch with myself and with my present and future relationships.

Just as I thought that the rain stopped, the sun came out and right there in front of me was a perfect rainbow, linking the sky and the Earth in this incredible arc. It seemed like everything good in the world and it gave me hope for the future

Experiences like these put a person on the threshold between ordinary and non-ordinary consciousness, the world around him and the spiritual connections between the two. Sometimes this threshold awareness can be liberating and enlightening, producing a much deeper understanding of oneself and one's path in life. That person's challenge now is to reconcile his experiences so he is able to integrate them, to build a new structure for his life in place of the old.

The quality that always shines in a true shaman is compassion for the paths that others must walk. This comes from the fact that the shaman has also walked through the underworld of the shadow and knows first-hand the pain involved in breaking the stranglehold of inner darkness

~ Jamie Sams

When the child returns to his tribe he has become a man. He has died in the sweatlodge, been reborn in the wilderness and fought for his life – his authentic, personal vision of life – during the quest itself. He returns with the victory of adulthood and has earned respect for the challenges he has faced and the battles he has fought. His return to the group and to feasting and celebration is his time of re-emergence into a new world.

A vision quest should be undertaken by everyone on the shamanic path, at least once. Normally it is taken for four days, in the way described above.

If this is a problem due to time constraints or other issues, however, then a night vigil can be an acceptable substitute to understand the spiritual nature of reality and to find your place within it.

Exploration: Making a Night Vigil

Spend a few days refining your thoughts so you are clear on the purpose for your vigil: to reach some decisions for yourself on how you want your life to be and the actions you need to take to change your future.

Begin the process by fasting for 24 hours before the vigil, drinking only mineral water during this time. Immediately before you begin, take a herbal bath to cleanse yourself (see chapter eight) and dress appropriately. Then walk out into Nature, to the location where you will undertake your quest. Purify and seal your space with incense or smudge mix and build a circle of stones around yourself.

Be aware of your thoughts and feelings during the vigil but do not give in to distractions or take notes; instead allow yourself to flow with your sensations. It may take a little time before you fully achieve this state of flow but go with it and don't give up. Find the threshold place within yourself, speak out loud to the spirits, ask for signs, omens or symbols from the natural world as to where your life should be taking you and what you were born to do. Use all of your senses and allow Nature to answer your call.

When the vigil ends – either at dawn or at the time you agreed with yourself that you would end it (and not at some new and arbitrary time which occurs to you during the process itself) – return home and take another bath, then change into ordinary clothes.

Now review the events of the last hours and write down your thoughts, feelings and experiences. Look at them again in a few days when they have had a chance to settle and begin to make new plans based on this information.

Quick Test 6

1. What is shamanic counselling? How is it done?
2. What is shamanic core process? How is it done?

3. List three types of divination with a brief explanation of each

Exercises

Continue to practice your journeying and dream work. Before you read the next chapter please also undertake these pieces of work which have a bearing on the subjects we will look at later.

1: Shamanic Counselling

Work with a friend and practice the technique of journeying for an answer to her questions, speaking your journey aloud. Do not select an extremely serious subject of enquiry but make it something that you can both check and validate in everyday reality.

2: Shamanic Core Process

Guide a friend through the stages of a journey to find her own spirit ally or power animal and to receive guidance from it. Discuss her journey with her and add further counsel from your intuition and guidance from spirit.

3: Divination

Choose one of the techniques of divination in this chapter and work with it either for yourself or a friend. Once again, make your question something that can be checked and validated in everyday reality.

Seven

Working with the Souls of the Dead

In this Chapter

The shaman as psychopomp, near-death experiences, hauntings and house cleansings, the healthy home, purifying your house, removing unwanted spiritual influences, protecting your home, cleansing buildings.

Reading for this Chapter

Life After Life (Raymond Moody)

Equipment Required

Drum
Drumming tape
Smudge stick
Other items as suggested in the text

The Shaman as Psychopomp

Because of his familiarity with the spirit world the shaman may be called upon in traditional societies to assist the souls of the dead to move on when they become trapped or lost or are in some way troublesome to the village. It is rarer in the modern world for a shaman to be asked to perform these duties (though it does happen). He or she may, however, be commissioned to work in a similar field – that of hauntings (typically of a property) or the removal of negative forces or realignment of energies within a house or workplace. In this chapter we look at these aspects: the shaman as psychopomp (conductor of souls) and the energetic cleansing of homes.

In traditional societies it was noticed that when people died, especially in sudden or violent circumstances, there was a tendency for their spirits to hang around. For example, after a battle with a rival tribe a village might experience unusual phenomena – the failure of crops, children having bad dreams, people seeing phantoms or strange lights and movements around them, and so on. The shaman would be sent on a journey to the spirit world to explore and find an explanation for these things and to resolve the situation if he could.

From these spiritual explorations shamans have arrived at a knowledge of the Land of the Dead, the needs of the souls who occupy it and the ways of helping them find peace beyond the human plane.

They discovered for example that when a person dies his spirit moves from the world of everyday reality into the middle world, the energetic dimension parallel to our own. (There is even some suggestion as to the weight of this soul: 21 grams, the amount that is mysteriously lost by the body at the point of death).

The soul remains in the middle world for a brief time until it is contacted by the spirits of ancestors, angels or allies who escort it to either the upper or lower world where it undergoes a life review, understands the lessons it came to Earth to learn and begins to settle into its new discarnate status.

The difference between upper and lower world as a final destination for this soul has nothing to do with the Christianised conception of good and evil (you don't go 'up to Heaven' if you have been 'good' and 'down to Hell' if you've been 'bad'); it is merely cultural convention. The shamans of different cultures, that is, believe that the Land of the Ancestors or the Dead is to be found in different places within the spiritual cosmology. In the Western world we tend to believe that the spirit first makes a horizontal transition from the ordinary middle world (the land of the living) to the spiritual middle world (the land of spirit or energy) and then a vertical transition upwards into the angelic realms (the upper world). In Haiti, after the initial horizontal movement the transition is downwards into the 'land beneath the waters' where ancestral spirits reside.

When this period of review and rebalancing is over the soul may move on into the continuing process of life-death-rebirth or, in some cultures, if the soul is very evolved and the person has acted during life in accordance with the will of God (the love-energy of the universe) it has a choice to escape this process altogether and become one with God, going back to the universal pool of energy from whence it started. The Christian philosopher Teilhard de Chardin called this 'merging with the 'Godhead''. Its parallel in the Buddhist tradition is the bliss state of nirvana where we become like a 'drop of water in an ocean', at one with everything.

Some spirits choose to do so but shamans tell us that others take pity on human beings because, having been human themselves, they recognise that being alive in this world is a difficult journey with sometimes hard lessons to learn and sorrows to bear. To support us they elect to become our allies instead. These are our tutelary spirits – the ones we have been working with during this book.

We in the West also know something of the stages of death from research that has been done into near-death experiences or NDEs.

Near-Death Experiences

The pioneer of such research is Dr Raymond Moody, who introduced the subject in his book *Life After Life* where he recorded and compared the experiences of 150 people who had died temporarily and then been revived. There are, he says, a number of things that occur in every near-death experience:

1. A sensation of being out-of-body, rising up and floating above the physical self and looking down dispassionately

at the 'shell' of the body while the self they now occupy is experienced as lighter and less-constrained. This sensation may be accompanied by a strange sound, described as buzzing or ringing, and a feeling of deep peace and contentment

2. A sensation of rushing quickly through a dark tunnel towards a source of light. Sometimes instead of going 'down' into this tunnel the person may float or be lifted 'up', looking back to the Earth

3. There is a meeting with wise and loving beings on the other side of the tunnel, entities that are perceived as the souls of relatives or friends (ancestors) who are there to greet them

4. There is then a period of orientation followed by a meeting with a spiritually powerful being who is understood to be the ruler of this realm and is sometimes described as God. This meeting inspires feelings of reverence or awe

5. This being presents the dead person with a detailed review of all they have done in their lives so they relive it and see how their life has been part of an intricate pattern. There may be a feeling of karmic learning associated with this – not a punishment or making amends but an opportunity for wisdom to be received (almost like a debriefing on the life experience)

6. Those who undergo this review and are revived return with the knowledge that love is the most important thing in the world

7. The emotions experienced in this Otherworld are often so intense and beautiful that there is a reluctance to come back. The Supreme Being, however, will advise the dead person that he must return, that it is not his time; or sometimes will offer him a choice to go or to stay. When they return it is normally because the near-death-experiencer senses a need from loved ones who are still living

and returns out of duty or compassion towards them.

There are of course obvious parallels with the shamanic experience – the journey through a tunnel or into the realms of sky beings to a spiritual landscape bathed in light; the out-of-body feeling of spirit flight; the meeting with guides and tutelary spirits who have an air of wisdom and compassion about them, and so on; giving credence to the shaman's assertion that the shamanic journey is not 'just' imagination, but a true out-of-body experience taken into the world of spirit.

Paediatrician Melvin Morse offers us further evidence, having spent almost 20 years studying near-death experiences in children. In 1982, while working at a clinic in Idaho, he was called to a young girl who had drowned in a swimming pool and had no heartbeat for 19 minutes. Miraculously, he was able to revive her and she went on to recover. Strangely, however, although dead at the time, she could recount the details of her resuscitation and told doctors that while she was 'away' she had been led through a tunnel to a place she called Heaven.

Interested in this account, Morse began a study of near-death experiences with children at Seattle Children's Hospital, comparing the experiences of 26 children who had been resuscitated after death with those of 131 who were severely ill and in intensive care but who were not near death.

His results showed that 23 of the 26 children in the near-death group (88%) had undergone experiences consistent with those identified by Raymond Moody as the near-death archetype, while none of the other children had.

Morse followed this research with a long-term study of these children, observing their progress as they grew up, compared with a control group who had not had near-death experiences. His results show that the survivors of near-death experiences have a much enhanced and richer experience of living as well as an appreciation of the sacred and of compassion in daily life.

Adult survivors of childhood near-death experiences are more likely to donate money to charity, to volunteer in the community, to work in the caring professions, to treat their bodies better and less likely to suffer from drug abuse or other social problems.

Almost every near-death experiencer reports a changed under-standing of what life is all about...Besides losing the fear of death a person may also lose interest in financial or career success. 'Getting ahead' may seem like an odd game that the person chooses not to play any more even if it means giving up friendships... Becoming more loving is important... They may seem to love everyone indiscriminately with no personal favourites... Deepened belief in God or a higher power is almost certain... Some people find they have an increase in intuitive or psychic abilities
~ International Association for Near-Death Studies

When we die, we become fully conscious, aware of our surroundings, and experience spiritual insights we do not often have at other times in our lives... We learn that human beings have an under-used area of the brain which is responsible for spiritual intuitions, paranormal abilities such as telepathy and remote viewing, and the power to heal not only the soul, but the body as well
~ Dr Melvin Morse

All of the above seems particularly true in circumstances where the person has an opportunity to adjust to their death or know that it is coming and can prepare for it. What shamans have discovered though is that when death is sudden, unexpected or has fear and trauma associated with it (such as a murder, a war or an accident) the person who has died can remain attached to the Earth because of the strong emotion that holds them there or because their death was so sudden that they literally do not know they have died.

Unfinished business is a major reason why spirits are unable to move on. In the sin eating tradition of Wales, for example, sins (things for which the person has not made amends) can become weights on the soul and these hold the spirit tied to the Earth.

Another form of attachment is addiction. Where a person has been a drug addict or alcoholic, for example, it may be that their craving holds them here so they can vicariously enjoy their physical pleasures through another. This is one of the reasons for possession. It also accounts for the high rate of reported pub hauntings, where spirits hang around the places where they were able to drink and experience high emotions (in fact, every place associated with heightened emotion – a theatre, cinema, castle, hospital and so on – is likely to have a higher chance of a haunting since the energies they contain draw the spirits to them).

In such situations of attachment the soul becomes confused, stuck, lost in the middle world or resistant to moving on. This is what shamans would find when they set out to explore the reasons for post-tribal conflict in the example given earlier. It then became the job of the shaman to release these lost souls so that peace was restored to the village. To do so he would journey to the middle world to find these souls and negotiate with them to move on. In this sense psychopomp work is soul retrieval for the dead.

Releasing Trapped Souls

As an example of the procedure let us use a case that you might come across in your shamanic work: a client who has recently lost her son in a car accident and who is now troubled by dreams of her child. What do you do?

Firstly, you may need to do some work for the woman herself to help her come to terms with her grief, to understand the nature of the spiritual universe that her son is now a part of (that he is not lost forever but part of an evolutionary process where he is now in the world of spirit) and/or to help her recover the soul parts she may have lost as a result of her trauma. Then you must help her son. This part of the healing process may have the following stages:

1. Preparation

Find out when and where the accident took place and if others were involved and died at the scene as well so you are not unexpectedly confronted with a group of distressed souls and a scene of chaos around you. Also find out the name of her son so you can call for him, along with any details and descriptions (a photograph is helpful) so you will recognise him in spirit.

2. Journeying

Journey to the scene of the accident and call for the lost soul by name. If you find him, first calm him down and help him understand what has happened. Reassure him that he will see his loved ones again and all will be well. If you don't immediately find him begin to work out in a spiral from the site of the accident. Sometimes souls go wandering in confusion. Look in particular for places with trees and water, which are gateways to transformation and will attract a confused soul. Other places to look are those of high emotion in the vicinity of the accident and in this case might include hospitals that the body of the deceased may have been taken to. Another place to look might be the destination the person was driving to (or from) when the accident happened.

3. Consultation and Negotiation

Once you have found the soul you are looking for and have him calm ask if he is ready to move on. It may be that he has a message for his loved ones, business to finish, things to let go of or that he requires healing for before he can do so. Do whatever is needed. Messages from the deceased can be a comfort to the living and offer proof that they are not gone forever so, *if it is appropriate,* as well as hearing the messages for loved ones it can be helpful to pass these on when you return from the journey.

4. Transition

At this point call on the assistance of your allies and power animals who are journeying with you and visualise a doorway or tunnel opening up in the space around you. There is light from this tunnel and as you watch it you will see spirits begin to move through it towards you. They are most likely the deceased relatives of the person you are working with but might also be angel-like beings. Guide the lost soul into the light where he will be greeted and comforted by these spirits. If other souls are present as a result of the accident work with them in exactly the same way.

5. Return

When this transition is complete visualise the doorway closing and return to ordinary consciousness. *If appropriate* pass on any messages to your client.

6. Client Work

Continue with any work needed for your living client, such as soul retrieval or power retrieval, or arrange a new appointment for her when this can take place.

Spirits of Place: Hauntings and House Cleansings

The souls of the deceased can sometimes find their way back to places they knew in life, typically where they experienced attachments and high emotions like those mentioned earlier and, of course, the home itself.

When we buy a house (especially an older one) we may therefore inherit these spirits. If they are not a disturbance to us and do not feel sorrowful or in need of help it is as well to leave them. They have a right to occupancy and in fact they were there first! If these spirits are distressed or troublesome, however, then the same procedure as for psychopomp work can be used to release them.

There is more to a healthy and happy home than this though because all things are alive to the shaman and of course all places naturally have their own energy too. This must be honoured and worked with if we are to live in harmony. This means understanding your home – not just as bricks and mortar but as a sacred space.

There is some interesting research on the power of place – negative as well as positive – from studies into the energy flows within houses. Scientists call this 'geopathic stress' and regard it, not as a spiritual disturbance of course, but a distortion of the Earth's electromagnetic field at certain locations. This distortion enables energies to be concentrated and rise up through buildings and other structures, causing tiredness, lack of energy and physical and emotional problems.

Research among 175 nomadic families, for example, found that people who were constantly on the move and not centred in buildings (like most of us are) were likely to suffer from cancer in less than 1% of cases. This is against a national average of 25%. The researchers suggest that illnesses like cancer can therefore be a disease of location. Nomads have a feeling for places which are free from geopathic stress they say (or as we might put it, they are more in tune with the energy or spirit of a place), but should they pick a bad spot they don't stay there long enough for it to harm them.

Other researchers have found that geopathic stress is the common factor in illnesses including MS, tuberculosis, meningitis, kidney and gallstones, rheumatism, heart and circulation problems as well as depression, insomnia, stress, high blood pressure, infertility, miscarriages, and in children with learning and behavioural difficulties. Two American doctors who studied 5,000 cancer patients to compare their sleeping positions with the intersection of energy lines in their homes found that in 98% of cases the point of origination of cancer in their bodies was at the exact position of the energy intersections that went across their beds. Another researcher in Australia found with 3,000 children diagnosed with Attention Deficit Disorder that simply moving their beds produced an improvement in their condition in 100% of cases.

We should not be surprised by these findings. Since the dawn of history shamans have been consulted over the suitability for occupancy of particular sites and would take into account the spiritual and energetic composition of the land (the spirit of place) in doing so as well as its visible physical features. Chinese shamans believe that spirits travel along straight paths, for example, and so would install winding routes up to the doors of temples and houses to prevent the entrance of negative energies. Similar methods of protection in the form of spirit gates called *torii* are installed before Japanese Shinto shrines. The Romans were also aware of the natural power of place and would leave cattle on a particular site before moving there themselves. They would watch closely to see what befell the herd and a year later would slaughter and inspect them to determine if the chosen site was healthy for human occupation.

These subtle energies in the air around us have a real impact on our lives. Journeying to the spirit of place is one thing you can do in your own home to understand its unique identity and to create a healthier and more energetic living space.

The Healthy Home

According to research into geopathic stress (or what the shaman will more likely call 'Earth medicine') there are a number of things you can do to ensure that the place you live in is healthy.

- Firstly, your surroundings should give a sense of harmony between yourself and Nature and there should be healthy trees and plants in your environment. The best type of atmosphere is one rich in the negative ions found near oceans and forests (trees and water once again, the great conductors of spiritual energies). The ground should be solid but not clay which encourages energy to seep away or sand which makes it difficult for energy to stabilise and settle. Your property should ideally face North or West and be situated as far as possible from power lines and other unnatural energy fields.

- Natural features such as hills and woodland behind the house are good signs but in front of the house they block energy flows. Streams, rivers and roads can have the opposite effect and should not flow directly towards you or you may be overwhelmed with energy and end up feeling 'on edge'.
- Natural construction materials such as wood and stone are preferable to man-made substitutes. For flooring, cork, wood and woollen carpets are much healthier than nylon and plastics.
- Areas where you will spend long periods of inactive time, such as the bedroom, should not be cluttered with electrical equipment such as clock-radios, TVs and stereos which release electromagnetic energy, soaking your body while you sleep. Always try to sleep with your head pointing North so you are aligned with the natural geomagnetic field of the Earth.
- Do not place furniture in an irregular way so as to block the flow of energy around your rooms. It is better to arrange chairs and tables in a circular formation.

Most of us do not live in the perfect house of course but there are remedial actions you can take to improve things. Always journey to the spirit of your house first though to find out what is best for the house itself since what is good for the building will also be good for those who live there. One simple thing you can do is walk the entire house using incense or smudge mix to clear out old energies and make your house your own. Clapping or ringing bells in the corners will also stir up accumulated and stagnant energy.

Feng Shui: An Early Shamanic Discipline

Like most things we could mention, before feng shui became a common new age practice it was a shamanic art. Shamans working in the home found that when they entered any room, with the door to their back, the areas of the room facing them from left to right in a circular pattern from where they stood represented the energies of the home owners in the following ways:

- Career
- Lifestyle
- Wisdom
- Wealth
- 'Fame' or spiritual illumination (what you make of yourself in life)
- Children and innocence
- Love
- The support of good friends
- The centre of the room is the point of tai chi or balance for the whole

If you are having problems or looking for improvements in any of these areas of your life some of the remedial actions suggested by these shamans (and now by feng shui experts) are as follows.

- If your stairs lead directly down to a front door place a mirror on the back of the door to reflect escaping energy which will otherwise flow out of the house.

- Place a wind chime or a crystal in your 'career' section to stimulate good energies at work.
- Ensure that whatever is placed in your lifestyle section reflects your ambitions and aspirations for your *whole* self. You may need to vision quest (see last chapter) or journey first to discover exactly what it is that you *do* want from life and the nature of your spiritual purpose in being here. In any case the needs that you have in response to this purpose are likely to change over time so whatever is in this corner should also be changed periodically.
- Place pictures of your relatives in the section corresponding to wisdom to ensure you have their support and spiritual guidance.
- Goldfish, plants and especially 'money plants', are recommended in the wealth section to encourage the free flow of good things towards you. A few coins left here or images of money are also helpful.
- In the 'illumination' section place candles or a mirror, anything reflective of you, or scrapbooks and other records of your achievements. This section is about you and the impact you will make in the world so it should reflect your true ambitions.
- In the 'children' section place images of your children. Light a candle here and relax so you can tune in to their childlike wisdom.
- In the 'love' section place photographs of loved ones, gifts and personal items they have given you, and so on. Lodestones, magnets and statues or images of lovers are also useful if you wish to draw new love into your life.
- In the 'friends' section place mementos of your friends or symbolic representations of their particular skills which may also be helpful to you.
- The key point in feng shui is not to live amongst clutter but to clean your rooms and keep them that way as clutter also

attracts spiritual energies, often of a negative kind.

In all of these teachings the fundamental discipline is to produce areas of focus and intention so that you can direct your will in these spaces to achieve the best results in your life. In a sense we create mini-shrines of intention in our rooms and when we light a candle there or see and hear a wind chime turning we are reminded and refocused on our intention. Clutter, by contrast, is a pool of unguided energy which is draining and pulls us away from the direction of our focus.

Explorations: A Healthy Home

1. Produce a 'feng shui' or energetic map of your house using the principles above.
2. Journey to make contact with the spirit of your house and enlist its support for your achievement of greater happiness, success or whatever else you may wish for.
3. Make some simple changes to the layout of your rooms or add items like those mentioned above (mirrors, candles, etc) to experiment with positive energy flows.
4. Pay attention to the changes that may result from this and adapt things as necessary.

New Orleans-Style Purification

In the New Orleans tradition there are additional practices for cleansing and purifying a home or business, some of which rely on plant spirit shamanism (which we look at in more detail in a later chapter). For example:

Purifying Your Home

Make up an equal quantity of dried basil and eucalyptus leaves and add a few drops of myrrh to the mix then set fire to the leaves, blow out the flames and walk the length of the house distributing the smoke in all rooms. This is a spiritual cleansing which restores 'lightness' to a house.

Nowadays, aromatherapy oils mixed together in a burner would do the job just as well as this traditional practice. It is your purifying intention which counts. Close all the doors and windows to ensure that the smoke (or oils) cannot dissipate and leave the house for a day. It will be purified on your return.

Removing Unwanted Spiritual Influences from Your Home

Rub a coconut with powdered eggshell and place it in the room farthest away from the front door. Kick or roll it through every room allowing it to fill up with any negative energies present until you get to the front door and then kick it out into the street. Repeat this exercise whenever you need to. This is similar to the idea of providing an alternative host for negative energies during spirit extraction work.

Protecting Your Home

Cut red, black and white thread into seven-inch sections then twist together three white strands, two black and two red and rub them with wax to stiffen them. You will need three of these multi-coloured ropes. Now heat three large iron nails in a fire until they are red hot and allow them to cool so they can be handled. Wrap each in the leaves of an onion or garlic plant and tie the package with the ropes. Then stand an ordinary egg in a bowl of sand and surround it with the wrapped nails. Keep this talisman in your home as a protective charm and feed it every day with a mixture of water and red wine.

A Framework for Cleansing Buildings

The shaman walks between worlds – which means that he or she has a role to play in both the spiritual and the material universe. If you are asked to help with a house cleansing, therefore, you will typically need to work in both dimensions. A structure for doing so might be:

1. Establish the Facts

Journey to investigate whether any deceased spirit is in occupancy and if so whether it is distressed or needs help to move on. If the answer is yes carry out psychopomp work as explained earlier. If the spirit is happy and not troublesome, however, there is no compulsion to release it. Instead you might choose to explain to the homeowners that this entity or energy is not problematic and in fact provides the building with blessings and protection if that is the case (which it often is). The owners might then need education in how to work with this spirit or at least give it the freedom it needs to co-exist peacefully with them.

2. Enlist Support

Journey to the spirit of the place (the natural energies of the environment or building) to ask if there is any work that needs to be done to assist natural and helpful energies to flow (is there geopathic stress present for example or anything else that needs to be considered? A pendulum will also help you to track the energies of a house and will spin appropriately – i.e. clockwise – if energy is flowing well but come to a standstill if stresses are present. This shows you where actions, such as those recommended by feng shui, may be needed.)

If unhealthy energies or stresses are present enquire of the spirit what can be done about them. Also refer to the practical suggestions from feng shui (see above) for how you can encourage positive forces to circulate and ensure they do not leave the house.

3. Take the Actions Required

Based on the information and advice you have received carry out the necessary actions. This may involve a ritual of some kind or a simple prayer for peace or blessing. It is also good practice, whatever else is advised, to use sacred sound (bells, chants, singing, etc) – especially in the corners of rooms where energy can stagnate – to get things flowing again. Ring a bell or clap your hands from ceiling to floor to stir things up. Then walk the rooms smudging and purifying the space.

Quick Test 7

1. What is a psychopomp and how does he or she work?
2. What is the typical structure of a near-death experience? In what ways is this similar to the shamanic experience of journeying or soul flight?
3. What is the spirit of a place? How is it helpful in rebalancing the energies of buildings?
4. Suggest three ways to stir up energy or get things moving in a building so it supports your intentions or those of your client
5. Describe one way of purifying a home

Exercises

Continue to practice your journeying and dream work. Before you read the next chapter please also undertake these pieces of work.

1. The Land of the Dead

Make a middle world journey to a place you know in ordinary reality that is somewhere with high emotions attached to it – a hospital for example – making sure you are fully protected and brimming with power before you do so. Your intention is only to explore this place, paying attention to the souls you may see here and your sense of their 'mood' or needs, but do not interact with them at this stage.

2. The Shaman as Psychopomp

Journey again to the same middle world destination, protecting yourself as before, this time with the intention of helping one soul towards the light. You may be asked for help by others and you have a choice to intervene and assist or not. If you elect to, do so on subsequent journeys. For the purpose of this exercise work with one soul only. Using the techniques in this chapter for releasing trapped souls, give the assistance required.

3. House Cleansing

Use the techniques in this chapter to carry out a spiritual cleansing of a friend's home. Journey to the spirit of place, smudge the rooms and use the principles of feng shui to energise and enliven them. If you sense the need, also carry out a purification. Enquire of your friend how things change both energetically and practically in the days after this work is done.

Eight

Plant Spirit Shamanism

In this Chapter

Teacher plants, ayahuasca: the vine of souls, icaros: the song of the universe, the leaf doctors of Haiti, explorations with plants, the bila – dreaming the spirit of the plants – the purification bath, journeying to the spirit of the plants, plant allies: sage, recipes for magical plant oils.

Reading for this Chapter

Plant Spirit Shamanism (Ross Heaven), *Plant Spirit Wisdom* (Ross Heaven), *Bartram's Encyclopedia of Herbal Medicine* (Thomas Bartram)

Equipment Required

None is essential but if you intend to make the plant mixtures and oils referred to in this chapter some items will be needed and these are explained in the text.

Teacher Plants

Life is everywhere. The earth is throbbing with it; it's like music.
The plants, the creatures, the ones we see, the ones we don't see;
It's like one, big, pulsating symphony.
~ Andrew Schneider

As we have seen, all shamans work closely with the spirits of Nature and as well as their skills with energy and spirit they are often accomplished herbalists or 'root doctors'. Once again, however, unlike conventional herbalists in the modern world, it is the plant spirit that the shaman works with not (just) the botanical or biochemical properties of plants.

There are many ways that he might work with these spirits. This chapter is an introduction to some of these and includes a series of exercises you can undertake to explore them and, having made your own connection to plant spirits, discover other ways of working with them for yourself. As the shaman-herbalist Loulou Prince says later in this chapter the way to really know the plants is to begin! And then, through your intuitions, dreams and journeys to find out more about them for yourself.

One of the ways the shaman works with plants is to regard them as his teachers, able to transmit not just healing information for clients but willing to act as allies for his deeper spiritual explorations. This is especially so when these plants are visionary (or as we in the West might say, psychotropic or hallucinogenic) in nature, such as peyote (used in the traditions of Mexico), San Pedro (used in the Andes) or fly agaric mushrooms (used in Siberia and other places in Europe). Another – nowadays famous – example of a teacher plant is ayahuasca, the vine of souls, which is used extensively in the Amazon regions. The importance of ayahuasca continues to grow in the West and you will no doubt hear more about it in the years to come so the first part of this chapter is an introduction to the plant and ways of working with it.

Ayahuasca: The Best-Known Teacher Plant

Ayahuasca is a shortcut. It's as if we had been travelling down the same highway as the rest of humanity but, in order to arrive at our destination more quickly we took a side road... a shortcut that leads us to truth.

~ Padrino Alex Polari de Alverga

Ayahuasca, the jungle medicine of the upper Amazon, is made from the ayahuasca vine (*Banisteriopsis Caapi*) and the leaf of the chacruna plant (*Psychotria Viridis*). Its ceremonial usage is as ancient as history itself. One of the oldest objects related to it is an engraved ceremonial cup found in the Ecuadorian Amazon which dates from 500 BC. This is now in the Ethnological Museum of Quito, Ecuador, and shows that ayahuasca was used at least 2,500 years ago.

The word ayahuasca comes from two Quechua words: *aya* meaning spirit, ancestor or soul and *huasca* meaning vine or rope – hence it is known as the 'vine of souls' although it also has many local names including yaje, caapi, natema, pinde, daime, mihi and dapa.

The plants are collected from the rainforest in a sacred way and it is said that the shaman finds the vine by listening for the 'heartbeat' that emanates from it. The vine is prepared by cutting it to suitable lengths, scraping and cleaning it, then pounding it to break it up. The leaves of another plant, chacruna, are picked and cleaned at the same time and added to the vine pulp. The whole mixture is then brewed and reduced for several hours until it becomes a thick brown liquid ready for drinking.

When this is taken in the correct ritual context the plant becomes a powerful ally that can open 'the doors of perception'. Every person who drinks will receive their unique experience of communion and healing from the plant spirit and the energies of the wider universe for which it acts as a gateway. This can be the start of a profound process of discovery and transformation which can continue indefinitely even if one never drinks ayahuasca again.

There are many legends about ayahuasca. One of the mysteries surrounding it for example is how the vine came to be used with chacruna leaves as the two plants always grow apart. According to Javier Arevalo, a shaman from the Peruvian Amazon, the answer is simple: ayahuasca itself told the shamans to add the leaves to the brew. Before this, ayahuasca was taken alone but in their visions the shamans saw that another plant (chacruna) was missing and asked how they could find it. The ayahuasca told them to go into the jungle and 'turn two corners'. They did so and saw a bush that attracted them. This was chacruna. Ayahuasca showed them how to find its 'soul mate'.

Icaros: The Songs of the Universe

Integral to an ayahuasca ceremony are the chants and songs of the shaman, known as icaros. These direct the visionary experience and the shaman has specific songs for each person's needs. Their purpose, in the words of Javier, is 'to render the mind susceptible for visions and healing'.

The words of the chants are symbolic stories telling of the ability of Nature to heal. For example, an icaro may tell of the power of a sacred stream to wash away illness or uncertainty or of brightly coloured flowers to attract hummingbirds whose delicate wings fan healing energies. What cures you, however, is the understanding ayahuasca brings of what is happening in your life, allowing inner feelings to unblock so that sadness or anger can change to ecstasy and love.

Some icaros call the spirit of ayahuasca to make the visions available, working on the optic nerves to render them able to *see*. Others call the 'doctors' – plant spirits for healing or animal spirits to protect and rid a person of 'bad magic' or spells. Icaros may also be used for specific conditions like manchare which a child may suffer when it gets a fright. The spirit of a child is not as fixed in its body as an adult's and a small shock can easily cause it to fly away (similar in a way to seiziman – see chapters four and five). Manchare is a common reason (in the Amazon at least) for taking children to ayahuasca sessions.

An important part of preparing for the ayahuasca experience is to undertake a period of quiet meditation and reflection on what you want the ayahuasca to do for you – the questions you want answering, the healing that you need. A special diet should also be followed for a few days before the experience which is intended to reduce excessive sugar, salt, oils, fats and spicy food. Pork in particular is avoided. Plainly cooked fish, fruits and vegetables are eaten instead. Sexual abstinence also forms part of the diet and is a traditional requirement of ayahuasca cleansing and healing. All of this will bring the ceremonialist into greater alignment with the spirit of the plant and open him up to its healing powers.

Leaf Doctors

In Haiti hallucinogens like ayahuasca do not form part of religious or spiritual practice but the way of relating to plants is very similar, demonstrating the same understanding of and respect for the powers of Nature.

Loulou Prince is a *medsen fey* (shaman and leaf doctor) for the coastal town of Jacmel close to the border with the Dominican Republic and in his daily practice deals with a range of health problems typical of the area – from cuts and bruises to more serious physical, emotional and spiritual complaints.

'The medsen fey is a person who knows how to talk to the spirits and to use leaves and other plant parts to promote health and cure illness,' says Loulou. 'Most people have some general knowledge of plants – for example, people in the West know that citrus fruits are good for colds and chamomile helps a person relax. Here in the Caribbean the plants are different but folk knowledge is passed along in the same way, by word of mouth, family recipe and by the spirits themselves.'

Often these spirits appear in dreams and advise the healer directly on the course of treatment to use with a particular client. 'I receive a lot of my knowledge in dreams,' says Loulou. 'If I am treating a sick person I ask for a dream where I see the leaves I should give that person. In these dreams the spirits come to me and tell me what to do or I see that I am in the woods and leaves are pushing up in front of me and these are the ones I should pick. Once I have this knowledge I can make a remedy for the person who is suffering.'

One of the most important of these spirits of the plants is Gran Bwa (a name which translates as 'Big Wood'). Gran Bwa is the spirit of the forests and all of their healing plants, herbs and trees. He is depicted in a *vever* (a mystical design used in Haiti to call the spirits) as a 'leaf-man' to show the intimate connection between human beings and Nature.

There are very few illnesses that cannot be healed with the plants of the forests (most of our modern pharmaceuticals are extracted from them). Loulou treats people with digestive disorders, sexual problems, fevers, colds and has medicines to clean and purify the blood and restore balance to the physical body. He also treats children who are not growing well due to persecution by evil spirits. Here the medicine is more magical in nature.

'There are specific leaves, strong-smelling leaves, which help children under spiritual attack. I mix these leaves with special magical items I have been shown by the spirits and then I take rum and sea water and make a bath for the child. I soak some of the leaves in rum and set them on fire to heat the bath up. Before I bathe the child I pray and bless the leaves. Then while I am bathing him I sing songs for the spirits and ask them to come and help this child. When that is done no one can curse that child or do evil to them.'

How this 'evil' comes to infect the child bears similarities to the almost universal belief in mal d'ojo, the evil eye. The magic comes through the judgements and jealousies of others and takes the form of a spirit intrusion or negative energy (see chapters four and five) that infects the victim.

As an example, Loulou was once asked to perform magical work for a woman who had four children, two of whom had died through the actions of evil spirits that would come to her house at night and suck the energy from them. The woman was a market trader who had been able to amass a little money (a rare commodity in Haiti) and her neighbours were jealous. 'One of them had sent spirits to kill her children,' said Loulou. 'I gave the child exactly what he needed. I bathed him and broke the bad magic. Then I gave him leaves to make his blood bitter so it would taste and smell bad and the spirits would go away. After that the child got better.'

In Haiti the blood (life force) can attract spirits who may use it to possess or infect that person, as was the case in Loulou's example of the sick child. A lot of the leaves that Loulou uses therefore have to do with the blood – 'building up the blood', cleansing it or making the patient 'throw off' blood. If she is pregnant for example with an unwanted child – a situation frequent in Haiti with a low uptake of contraception and sufficient poverty to make large families untenable – Loulou has medicines to help her painlessly abort the child by changing the spiritual constituents of the blood which reaches the foetus. It then becomes less attractive to the spirit of the growing child to be in the womb and its soul returns to the Otherworld where it is welcomed back by the ancestors.

Magical healing in Haiti is often for very practical purposes like these or for drawing in money, protecting livestock, blessing a marriage, keeping a lover faithful, and so on. There is no division, in the Western sense, between good health and good 'luck' – if you are in control of your life and the things around you, you are automatically power-full and it is more difficult for the spirits to enter your body and harm you – which is what we also found in our discussion of power and power retrieval in earlier chapters.

The Bila: For Dreaming the Spirit of the Plants

Everyone has their own spirits and they can help you. Maybe they will come to you in dreams and tell you things that will help you.
    ~ Loulou Prince

In Haiti, the bila is a ceremonial pillow which is stuffed with aromatic herbs. An initiate into the shamanic tradition will kneel before the bila and beat it with a machete for hours on end as one of his initiatory tests. This releases the aroma of the herbs and through a combination of exhaustion and the effect of these herbs the initiate will enter a trance state where the spirits can talk to him.

Many people in the West understand that herbs can influence us subtly in ways like this and may sleep with a pouch of lavender next to their bed, for example, or with rose or primrose-scented sheets to relax them and change their mood in slight but perceptible ways. The herbs of the bila are in this respect no different and you can create a bila for yourself, using Western herbs, in order to stimulate your dreams and open you up to the spirit of the plants so that, as Loulou says, these spirits can 'come to you in dreams and tell you things that will help you'.

One recipe for a bila is to take small handfuls of dried marjoram, rosemary, sage, fennel and geranium petals and mix them together. Sprinkle the mixture with neroli, orange and patchouli (aromatherapy oils are fine) and a little rum and water until it becomes sticky. Put your intention into this – that these herbs will help you sense a new order to the universe and the spirit of the plants will guide you in your dreams. Allow the mixture to dry for a few days in a place where the sun and the moon will both shine on it. When it is dry crumble it into a pouch and place it beneath your pillow.

When you go to bed that night pray that the spirits come to you and teach you the nature of the spiritual universe or answer any questions you have as you sleep. You can also make a request for healing or for love – or anything else you need. Keep your dream journal next to your bed and as soon as you wake up next morning immediately note down your dreams and first waking sensations. Repeat this ritual for a few weeks then dispose of the bila and make up a fresh herbal mixture if you wish to continue.

A similar method for inducing dreams that will impart specific information or healing on a soul level comes from the Hindu tradition which uses a dream pillow. Making a dream pillow is like weaving a spell because again you must concentrate on your intentions while making the pillow. The herbs that you use are, in this tradition, determined by which facets of your life you need guidance with. The list below offers some correspondences to the spices, herbs and flowers that are often used. For information on:

- Love: use rose and/or cinnamon
- Money: bergamot
- Health: fennel or lavender
- Stopping nightmares: cloves
- Spiritual development: jasmine

Set the atmosphere by lighting a plain white candle, some incense and by stating your intention for the sort of dream you want to have. This can be for specific guidance or to re-visit a dream you have had previously, for example.

Cut a piece of natural cloth (silk or cotton is fine) into a rectangular shape about twice the width of a CD case. Black or white are good colours for this but you can also choose colours appropriate to your own emotional responses or tastes.

Fold the rectangle in half so it forms a square. Sew up two sides of this square while holding your intention in your mind then turn the sleeve you've created inside out. Fill the pillow with a 'hot' base spice such as ajwain (obtainable from Indian greengrocers or larger supermarkets in the spice section) and then add the flowers and herbs most appropriate for the area/s in which you want guidance. Neatly sew up the top and you will have a small square pillow.

Again state your intent and put the package under your

pillow and sleep that night on it. You will have a significant dream based on your intent. The next day write down the dreams you remember. Don't interpret them straight away though; ponder them for a week or so instead. An intention for dreams based on love is best made on a waxing moon and dreams on health are best on a waning moon.

The Purification Bath

Another traditional way of working with plants is to use them in a special bath, as Loulou relates. This recipe, also from Haiti, is dedicated to and works with the energy of Erzuli, the spirit of love. You can take this bath any time you feel the need to cleanse yourself of negativity or stress – after a hard day at work or an argument, for example – and to draw in love and luxury. It also gives you a basic formula and approach around which to start devising your own healing baths (also see the section on magical oils later in this chapter) so you can make formulas for your clients or yourself. For the Erzuli bath you will need the ingredients below, as fresh as possible and of the best quality you can afford.

- Two or three sprigs of basil
- A handful of rose petals (and/or a few drops of rose aromatherapy oil)
- Four or five leaves of lettuce
- A few cuttings of fresh aloe (and/or a small cup of aloe juice)
- Four or five orange leaves (and/or a few drops of orange aromatherapy oil)
- A few drops of Florida Water (or perfume)
- A glass of champagne (or good quality sparkling wine)
- One small can of evaporated milk
- Three or four drops of vanilla extract
- A glass of coconut milk

- Four rose quartz crystals
- A pink or white candle

All herbal ingredients except the rose petals are ground together and added to a basin of warm water then allowed to soak for an hour or so for their essence to infuse it. Then strain out the plant material and pour the water along with the other liquid ingredients directly into your bathing water. Scatter the rose petals on the surface and place the rose quartz crystals around the bath, one at each corner.

Turn out the lights and bathe for a while by the light of the candle. Ask as you do so that Erzuli blesses the water and empowers it to refresh and cleanse you spiritually so you attract happiness, luxury, love and abundance into your life. When you are ready, get out of the bath and dry yourself with a clean white towel. Do not use deodorant. Dress in clean white clothes. If any of the rose petals remain on your skin or hair allow them to stay there until morning. There should be no sex on the night of your bath and preferably no contact with any living soul.

In the morning take the remnants of your bath (the crushed plants and candle) and bury them at the base of a tree. The quartz crystals can be washed in salt water and dried in the sun for later use.

Journeying to the Spirit of the Plants

In both the Amazon and Haiti it is the plants themselves – or rather their spirits – that tell the shaman how they are to be used. This is as true for medsen fey Loulou Prince who dreams the healing properties of various forest species as it is for the ayahuasca shamans who were told by the vine how to find its mate, chacruna, and create the visionary brew.

In fact, by tuning in to the plants it becomes obvious that we know far more about their qualities than we think we do. For this exercise choose one or two herbs that you would like to know more about but have little information on at present then work with them in the following ways:

- Spend some time gazing the plants, merging your consciousness with them to sense their qualities and healing intentions.
- After you have spent time with a particular plant, gazing it, smelling it, tasting it and exploring it in other ways through your senses begin to write, as a stream of consciousness, all the ideas and associations that come to you when you think of this plant.
- Then journey to the spirits of your plant to meet it and enquire about healing properties and the ways these manifest in the plant itself.
- Gather all of this information together and refine it so you come up with a 'specification' for the herb you have chosen in a similar way to the example below (The section on 'spiritual intention' is the most important).

Example: The Spirit of Sage

Collection: Leaves can be harvested at any time but are more potent in spring.

Healing Actions: Antiseptic and cleansing – will disinfect open wounds and kill intestinal worms. Used in a burner or boiled in water it cleans the air, hence its use in sickrooms to kill viruses, etc. It is also an essential ingredient for mouthwash and toothpastes and will heal throat infections, mouth ulcers, tonsillitis, etc.

Spiritual Intentions – what the sage has to say (based on a journey to its spirit): Sage is for drying and protection. It is a sacred plant also used in cleansing and spellcraft. It can be used for magical protection by growing it at the entrance to the home or using it in sachets suspended over the doorway. Dreams and divination are enhanced when sage is used. The aroma is said to resemble the fragrance of wealth so it can also be used in money rituals. It establishes a sacred boundary at the beginning of rituals and ceremonies (the sacred pipe of the Sioux is kept in a bundle of sage). Its tongue shape indicates its use for mouth infections. Its name ('sage') suggests wisdom – and it will help restore failing memory.

Once you have assembled your information like this on the plant of your choice check your intuitive sense against the information in an herbal encyclopaedia to see how your assessment compares with other experts (I recommend *Bartram's Encyclopedia of Herbal Medicine* because it is comprehensive but easy to use for quick reference). You may be surprised at how accurate you are. But in fact this is not so amazing if you think about it because sometime, somewhere, the spirit of the plants must have told someone their secrets so they could be recorded in an encyclopaedia at all so why shouldn't they also speak to you?

Magical Oils

Plants are also used in the creation of oils with special properties for the attraction or repulsion of certain qualities. In the Hoodoo tradition of New Orleans, root workers noted the spiritual affects of these plants on the energy body and how they did more than heal or impact the physical self but could actually change luck or quality of life. From this they produced a range of magical oils with properties that people most needed or requested from them. Here is a selection of these oils that you can create for yourself and either wear or use as instructed to bring you the things you most need. In all cases (unless otherwise stated) use grape seed as the carrier oil and add essential oils in the quantities stated.

Air elemental oil

To promote clear thinking, for protection during travel and to overcome addictions.

5 drops Lavender

3 drops Sandalwood
1 drop Neroli

Earth elemental oil
For grounding and stability and to bring money and abundance.
4 drops Patchouli
4 drops Cypress

Fire elemental oil
For passion and to lift the spirits.
3 drops Cinnamon
12 drops Orange
2 drops Clove
7 drops Nutmeg

Water elemental oil
For love, healing, psychic awareness and purification.
3 drops Palma Rosa
2 drops Ylang-ylang
1 drop Jasmine

Temple oil
Enhances spiritual connection and the power of ritual magic.
4 drops Frankincense
2 drops Rosemary
1 drop Bay
1 drop Sandalwood

Anointing oil
For the ritual anointing of magical objects.
5 drops Sandalwood
3 drops Cedarwood
1 drop Orange
1 drop Lemon

Moon oil

To induce psychic dreams, speed healing and aid sleep.

1 drop Jasmine

1 drop Sandalwood

Sun oil

For healing, vitality and strength.

4 drops Frankincense

2 drops Cinnamon

1 drop Petitgrain

1 drop Rosemary

Summary: Ways of Working with Plant Spirits

In this chapter we have looked at a few of the ways that plants can be used to heal, expand consciousness and bring more wide-ranging practical results. In fact, the only limitation to the use of plants is your imagination because once you form a connection to these spirit energies they can be used in numerous ways, not only those we are familiar with in the West.

All shamans agree that the way to learn about plants is to spend time with them and make contact with their spirits who (like all spirits) will then offer you personal training and insights into their uses. This chapter has hopefully opened your mind to some of these uses but you are encouraged to take your own explorations further by forming a deeper connection to the spirit of these healing allies by journeying to the plant spirits themselves.

Quick Test 8

1. What is ayahuasca and why is it a teacher plant?
2. What *is* a teacher plant? What distinguishes it from any other?
3. What do Amazonian shamans mean when they talk of a plant diet?

4. What is a medsen fey and how might he receive plant information from the spirits?

Exercises

Continue to practice your journeying and dream journal work and also undertake these next pieces of work.

I. The Icaro

Icaros are power songs given to the shaman by the spirits of the plants. They can be sung into the body of a client to provide her with the healing power of that plant even if the plant itself is not physically used. Singing these songs also helps the shaman strengthen his partnership with the spirit of a particular plant.

For any herb that interests you spend some time gazing it and journeying to it so you come to know its spirit then ask for an icaro or power song that encompasses its spirit so you can use it in your healings.

2. Plant Counselling

Make a lower world journey to meet your power animals. Ask their advice and recommendations on a particular herb that would be of value in your healing or spiritual development and how this should be used (in a bath, as a drink, etc). Also check this information in an herbal encyclopaedia.

If there are no contraindications (and if you are happy to do so) diet this plant for a week and see if you notice any beneficial health effects or other changes in your life. (Stop the diet immediately if you do not feel comfortable or if you notice any effects you are not happy with). A diet is taken by eating bland food and avoiding spices, pork, salt, sugar, lemons and limes, alcohol, and restricting your sexual behaviours. On top of this eat or drink as a tea the herb or plant you have chosen as your ally, once a day for the first three days, but continue the other dietary restrictions for a further four days.

3. Using Herbs

There are many ways that herbs can be taken (for example, as teas, infusions in alcohol, gargles and mouthwashes, etc). Practice preparing herbs or herbal mixtures recommended to you by spirits as teas and infusions.

Tea: Place a teaspoon or two of herbs in a piece of muslin and tie up the ends with string. Add hot water and honey to taste. (You can also add herbs in muslin bags like this to bath water so the herbs infuse your bath).

Infusion: Add the herbs to alcohol (vodka is often used and the shaman may also blow smoke into the mixture as a carrier for healing intention) and allow them to steep for a few weeks. Take a few spoonfuls a day as a tonic. (Again, if there is any effect you are not happy with discontinue your practice).

Nine

Ethics
Working with Clients and Issues in Modern Shamanism

In this Chapter
Client awareness and feelings, healer intentions and preparations, healing procedure, issues in modern shamanism: Should shamanic healing be free? Sex in healing. Legal issues. Insurance.

Suggested Reading
None

Equipment Required
None

If you have followed the lessons and exercises in this book it may be that you are now considering working with clients of your own. Before you do so I would like to offer a word on this and about some of the issues you might face when dealing with clients or in modern shamanic practice in general.

Client Awareness and Feelings
Although awareness of shamanism is growing in the modern West clients may still have little idea about what shamanic healing actually entails – even if they have contacted you and asked to receive it! They may even be wary of it after some of the things that get written in the press about 'new age cults', 'oddball healers' and 'charlatans' (i.e. basically anyone who doesn't fit the mainstream medical model.)

The fact that a client may be wary and still coming to see you, however, is indicative in itself of her deep need for healing. Especially if she has no previous experience of shamanism, it is very courageous of her to take the step of coming to a healer and in fact it is an act of power on her part.

On her way to see you she may feel strange, more aware of herself and her emotions or more deeply connected to her inner world than is usually the case. Good! This is exactly what you want.

Before I see a client I ask her to think about her problems or concerns and the outcome she would like and to write this down and bring it with her so she doesn't forget – because I *want* her to engage with her healing and shift her attention away from the everyday world. (The list she creates can also be placed on the altar in my healing room to strengthen the connection to spirit and provide a link between her and the spirit world).

When we perform any healing, that is, we are aiming to shift our client's consciousness into a slightly altered state so she can receive new energies ('altered' in this context, by the way, means 'free of the everyday trance we have all been socialised into and which has now become our habit'). Your client will already be starting this process during her journey to you and you should bear this in mind and support it. At the very least it means she'll be better able to talk about her feelings and fears when she arrives because she'll be in a different space from 'normal'.

Healer Intentions and Preparations

Part of your intention as a healer should be to build on this change in your client so she can get further in touch with herself, so prepare your healing room with this in mind, ready for when she arrives. Try to create an 'otherwordly' feel to it so you're supporting her subtle shift in awareness. This may mean incense and candles (more relaxing and healthy than electric light anyway), exotic throws and prints – things that create a different-to-usual impression without veering into flakiness.

Things that will put her at ease (such as any healing qualifications you have for example) will also help by making your skills and credentials obvious. Medical doctors do this all the time – their props are white coats and stethoscopes, medical books and, of course, their title and qualifications.

There are also some things you need to prepare in advance which aren't props but tools of the healing trade. So the healing goes smoothly and without need for interruptions make sure you have:

- A blanket and pillows for your client to lie down on
- Smudge mix or incense to purify the space and a holder for this
- A lighter or matches for the smudge and candles
- Your rattle
- Your drum and/or drumming tape

Optionally also:

- A selection of feathers (and/or an egg) in case extraction work is necessary
- At least four quartz crystals, a pendulum and a collection of stones (for energy rebalancing and mapping the energy body)

Healing Procedure

These suggestions are based on a typical healing practice. You will of course find your own way in consultation with spirit and what works for you but these may be useful guidelines until you find your own procedure.

I. Before Your Client Arrives

Begin by smudging the room, the tools you will use, and yourself. As you cleanse each ask its spirit for help in the healing.

Everything is alive and has the right to be asked and invited in.

You also need to feel powerful yourself, especially if you're likely to be dealing with spirit intrusions. A reminder: There are a number of ways to call in power:

- Journey to your power animals and ask for their help with the healing;
- Drum, sing, meditate or dance yourself into trance to connect to your allies
- Ensure you have a strong bond to your allies in Nature that will take any intrusions into their care. One way to do so is by visualising them through use of your active imagination

When you have done all of this sit down and relax in a meditative state so you don't lose your connection to power and await your client's arrival.

2. Pre-Client 'Nerves'

There are many new shamans – certainly those first starting out as healers – who think to themselves 'I can't do this; I'm not a real healer!' as they await the arrival of a client. And they're right – *they* can't do it because they aren't the real healers, their spirits are. As long as you bear this in mind healings become much easier because then you have nothing to 'prove'; you are merely the conduit for spirit.

Nerves can be natural but if you begin to have real doubts about your ability to heal it suggests that you are not fully connected to power and your ego is creeping back in. This is a signal to do more work on calling in power so you can get your ego out of the way and become a 'hollow bone' for the spirits to heal through.

3. When Your Client Arrives

Welcome your client and chat for a few minutes to set her at ease.

As you do so watch her and listen closely to what she says. This may give you some clues as to the real or underlying nature of the problem she needs help with, given that most people are not particularly connected to what is fundamentally wrong for them or the patterns that they are part of so may not be able to express these clearly to you. Obvious examples include:

- She says: 'I really love my mother…' Listen for the '… but', even if she never says it. Is it there somewhere, spoken silently? Might this suggest a problem with power or even soul loss?

- She says: 'I've never been happier than in my current job.' But notice how she wrings her hands as she says it. What might that mean?

- Where do her eyes go as she speaks? If down and to the left she is often remembering something; if up and to the right she may be imagining something or she's not sure about it but it might have happened and you should treat it as if it did unless your spirits say otherwise.

- How is she breathing? High up in her chest may suggest fear as she talks about a particular issue (fear or anxiety probably means an issue to do with power loss); low in her stomach may suggest grief (and this might imply the need for a releasing ritual). You will form your own relationship with the breath as you continue your work and come to understand what these clues mean to you.

- If she mentions a problem with her back in my experience this may suggest a feeling of betrayal (being stabbed in the back) and usually relates to an event which has happened some time ago (it is behind her). This normally means a family issue, probably related to her childhood.

- If she has a headache or feels under pressure this may suggest a problem with the energy body. Most likely it is too close in to her physical body and as energy grows denser under pressure it gathers more mass and becomes more solid. People with compressed energy bodies often feel under threat from what is happening around them and try to make themselves 'small' to avoid attacks from their environment. Also ask her if she feels heat and/or sluggishness in her body which can also happen when the energy body is compressed.

These and other observations will help you to help her by getting an intuitive sense of the problem which a client may not be able to vocalise.

While you are doing this also use your powers of gazing to *see* your client. As you talk allow your eyes to go slightly out of focus and use your peripheral vision to look just past her. What do you see in her energy body? What images enter your mind which are relevant to what might be going on for her? Trust your first impressions. Once you start telling yourself 'that can't be right' your rational mind will begin to get in the way and that's when you can lose your connection to power.

If you see something clearly in her energy field, even at this stage you *might* want to raise it with your client – *but only if you can do so sensitively and if it is appropriate.* This can add a new dimension to the consultation and get you closer to the heart of the problem, but again, sensitivity to your client's feelings and concerns is paramount. I once saw a grey mist over the face and chest of a client for example and mentioned it to her. It turned out she'd had a breathing problem since early childhood. Through our ensuing discussion it became apparent that this problem arose from a suffocating home environment and the loss of power this entailed. Once we understood its nature the intrusion could be removed and her problems disappeared.

4. Beginning the Healing

After you have chatted for a while take your client into your healing space, let her lie down and relax. Make sure your hands are clean (spiritually as well as physically) as you are about to touch her soul (literally). Oil of frankincense is a good purifier and (unless you are in any way allergic to it) can be simply rubbed on your hands. Then smudge your client and begin your work (see earlier chapters for one method of smudging).

5. Proceed with the Healing in the Way You Practiced in Earlier Chapters

This is likely to involve:

- Energy rebalancing using crystals, stones and a pendulum
- Spirit extraction: the removal of energies which are not serving her
- Power retrieval
- Soul retrieval in more serious cases
- Sealing your client's energy body (through the use of the rattle)
- Thanking the spirits and closing the healing

6. After the Healing Session

Pass on any spirit counsel you have received and explain to your client (again, with sensitivity) what you have done for her and anything she can now do to continue the healing you have begun. Bear in mind my earlier comments that it is not always good practice to tell a client the exact form taken by any intrusive energy or entity you have removed. This is a judgement call every healer must make but your main concern should, of course, be to ensure you do not cause your client distress.

I normally make myself available to a client for a few weeks after a healing to support her in case new memories, insights or information arise during this time. It can be the case when energy is moved around that a new understanding begins to surface and/or other changes take place over the course of a few weeks and it may be that the client wants to check things out with you or ask for further advice. It is not, however, suggested that you enter into lengthy discussions with any client about the 'meaning of things' or the nature of the power you returned etc, which some clients will ask you to do. This is the rational mind at work and its need to 'understand' whereas shamanic healing comes (almost by definition) from the irrational: the world of spirit. 'Explanations' can therefore block the healing and it is better for your client to simply allow her new energy to flow and her emotional self to feel the impact of the healing.

I also suggest the client leaves it a few weeks for her energies to settle before she makes major life changes that the healing may have suggested to her, and that she is as gentle and forgiving with herself as she can be during this time. She should also drink plenty of water to assist her new energies to flow, get as much sleep as she needs and take time out in nature. After a few weeks I ask her to let me know how she feels and if she wants to make another healing appointment. This puts the power back into the client's hands for her own healing, which is different again to the Western medical model but is how it should be.

Issues in Modern Shamanism

There are a number of issues and debates in modern shamanism which confront practitioners, as well as legal considerations they must be aware of. These are some of those now current, but you should also keep an eye on current affairs to see how other changes in law or opinion may affect you.

Should Shamanic Healing Be Free?

This is a question which comes up from time to time in healing and especially, for some reason, in shamanic healing: the suggestion being that practitioners should donate their time and skills to others or give their services free, not as a matter of choice but a matter of course.

In fact, although it is expressed as a question, it is really a statement or an implied judgement which, once elaborated, goes like this: 'How can you charge for something so vital? Healing is a gift that should be available to all. The shamans in traditional tribes don't charge for healing, they give their help freely to others so either:

(a) you should do the same,
(b) you are exploiting the knowledge of traditional people for your own ends and should be ashamed of yourself and/or
(c) you are a 'plastic shaman'/fake shaman/not real.'

It's a judgement that comes and goes like a fashion but one which practitioners are hearing again these days as the financial recession deepens. I suspect that the two are related: a greater need for personal healing as a result of the problems of the world and less money to pay for it as a result of those same problems, leading to frustration or anger towards healers who appear to have the answers but whose services are beyond financial reach.

I have a lot of sympathy for people in need of healing and who *genuinely* cannot afford to pay for it but less so for the idea or expectation that healers *must* or *should* give their time, energy – and, yes, income – away to a prospective client in order to solve their problems for free. These are my counter-arguments.

'How can you charge for something so vital that people need?'
Do you charge for what you do? If you have a job do you take a salary or do you give your time and skills to your employer for free? If you are not working do you claim welfare benefits? So who pays for those and what are you giving back in return?

In the Western world money is the predominant method for exchanging energy and all of us – including healers – use it in one way or another for the purchase of goods and services which are also vital to life, such as food, heat, clothes and shelter. All things have a cost so on what basis should healing be any different? If your answer is 'a moral one' then, again, what is the moral difference between a healer charging for services and an electricity company charging you for heat and power since both are essential for health and well-being?

Healers are not immune to the need for heat and power or to the need to feed and clothe their children and they are not exempt for paying for these services. Sadly, they have no magic wands which will make their tax demands and water bills disappear. Just like you they need money to pay for these things because if they cannot then soon they will not be able to offer healing of any kind or at any price to anyone.

The answer to the question 'How can you charge?' is therefore a simple one: 'Because I have to – just like everyone else. The minute that money ceases to be the commodity of exchange and the world finds some other method for healers to pay their ways I am sure they will embrace it.'

There will, however, always be a need for payment of some kind. Was it Mark Twain who defined a cynic as someone who knows the cost of everything and the value of nothing? Cynicism is a state of mind we can easily fall into when anything is given to us for free. As a young psychology student I carried out an experiment once where I tried to give away £5 notes. Most people wouldn't take them because of the sheer fact that they were free and this meant that they lacked intrinsic value since they hadn't been worked for and had no power, worth or energy attached to them.

In healing, energy and power is everything. Clients must be engaged by the healing and play their part in it too if they are to be made well. A 'free' healing lacks value. We suspect that 'it can't be worth much if they're giving it away' and we treat it with suspicion. Since we invest nothing in it, nothing may be what we get from it.

Free healings, while they may lack value very often have a cost, however. I'm thinking of the days when I used to offer presentations and seminars at festivals and gatherings. It was not unusual at these events for someone – often an enthusiastic and well-meaning amateur – to bound up and give me a 'free healing' even though I'd not asked for – and didn't want – one! It usually transpired that these were people who had just 'seen the light' and stepped onto the healing path and while their intentions were genuine I would sometimes be left with the impression that their ego-needs were being most served: that by healing me they positioned themselves as healers. The cost to me was time and energy and the suspicion that I'd just been used as a practice dummy even though I didn't have to pay for the healing I received.

I hope that doesn't sound too cynical, but then that's often the situation with a 'free healing': that we are left feeling cynical about it instead of actually healed.

'Healing is a gift that should be available to all'

Is healing a gift? The word implies a special talent that is given only to a select few. My view is that healing is an innate ability given to us all; it is just that most people choose not to nurture or develop it or to acknowledge their own talents.

Those who do and who go on to become good healers often have to put themselves through hardships and financial or other costs in order to recognise and refine their skills, just as a student with an innate gift for mathematics will most likely have to pay his way through university before he can make the most of his abilities.

In the case of shamanic healers training often means travelling to learn from shamans in other cultures, serving apprenticeships or investing in workshops and courses, sometimes for several years – or at least buying a book like this – before they consider themselves (or are considered by others) to be effective healers.

In my case, by way of example, I met my first shamanic teacher at the age of eight and spent more than 10 years learning from him. I then went to university and studied psychology, sociology, philosophy and other subjects which could help me put into context and consolidate what I had learned from him. After this I travelled and worked with shamans in other cultures including the Amazon, Andes and Haiti as well as taking workshops and courses with Western teachers. Only in my 30s did I begin as a fulltime healer myself and by then I had invested thousands of pounds as part of an education in healing which had already taken me more than 20 years.

This is far longer than a Western medical qualification, by the way, and yet no-one objects to paying their doctor for medical advice or treatment or for prescriptions and medicines. By the same token we may not enjoy paying the bills of other professionals like accountants and solicitors but most of us accept that we must.

'Shamans in traditional tribes don't charge for healing'

Really? I am constantly amazed by this statement (which is frequently made by people who've never actually met a 'real' shaman, whatever they perceive that to be). I have sought out and studied with shamans from many different countries over several years and can say, hand on heart, that I have *never* met a healer who gives their services free of charge. All of them believe in the principle of reciprocity (energy exchange) which they regard as a fundamental law of the universe.

In those countries where money is the commodity of exchange the prices of some shamans can be high, especially when Westerners are paying for treatments. Like the plant doctor I worked with in Haiti who charges $350 US for a week's work. That's $50 a day! You might wonder why I'm so amazed at that when a new pair of boots or a haircut can cost twice as much in the UK or America – until you realise that the average *annual* wage in Haiti is around $350 US so in the terms of his culture he's charging the equivalent of around $40,000 for a week's work.

In those cultures where money is less important the shaman may be paid in other ways. Where food is scarce and has a high relative value, for example, he or she might be paid in rice or chickens or wine. This is also common in the rural communities of Haiti where a farmer may not make much money but will have produce for exchange and healers, of course, need to eat. There is, however, *always* a payment of some kind.

'[Shamans in other cultures] give their help freely to others so either

(a) *you should do the same,*

(b) *you are exploiting the knowledge of traditional people for your own ends and should be ashamed of yourself, and/or*

(c) *you are a 'plastic shaman'/fake shaman/not real'*

Maybe we've answered this argument above: traditional healers do not – *ever* – give their services free. It's a Western stereotype or myth that they do but it's completely false. But even if it were true it does not mean that healers in the West *must* do the same. Our predominant reward and exchange mechanism is money (as opposed, for example, to the almost-mythical 'pinch of tobacco' or bag of rice) and if energy exchange is the key universal principle in shamanism then in this respect money is as good as anything. It is a symbol of the reciprocal relationship between healer and client, man and God, Earth and universe.

There is no compulsion on the part of Western healers to take money in exchange for their services of course (you might, for example, offer healing in exchange for the provision of goods and services to a similar value, which is the basis for many Local Energy Trading Systems – and ask for your gardening or plumbing to be done instead by a suitably qualified client) – but nor should healers feel compelled to reject money if that is more useful or conducive to their ways of life.

Let's move on to part (b) of this statement ('you are exploiting the knowledge of traditional people for your own ends') and pose some questions in response.

What is exploitative about paying someone to give you knowledge and training? If we attend a Western university we pay our teachers through tuition fees and the situation is precisely the same with traditional shamans. All those I have worked with have, without exception, been paid for the training and services they provide and in the ways they wished to be paid. What *would* be exploitative I believe is to benefit from their healings and training and *not* pay them in the expectation that they *should* (according to the Western stereotype) give us training or healing for free.

The idea of exploitation raises another question which is also interesting to ponder without judgement: If these traditional shamanic teachers are prepared to pass their knowledge on to us (which may not have been theirs in the first place but passed down through the generations) for a fee, who are the actual 'exploiters'? Us for paying them for tuition or them for selling the ideas and heritage given to them by somebody else? The real question I suppose is 'Who owns knowledge?'

Then, having received this wisdom and training what should we do with it? To avoid accusations of exploitation should the shamanic healer refuse to use it and let it die out instead? To me that seems pointless, of no use to those who require healing and wholly against the wishes of those who have taught us to start with. Does anybody ever teach anything so it can be monopolised and controlled by the one person who receives it (if so why not simply hold onto it yourself and be that one person) or abandoned and left to die? Did your teacher in high school go to the effort of teaching you politics or history or mathematics so you could ignore every lesson and throw your notes away?

Shamanic knowledge applied to healing is never for the benefit of the healer, just as training in Western surgery is never for the benefit of the surgeon. It is a skill to be used to help others and there is absolutely no shame in it or in being rewarded for it.

So, are we 'plastic shamans'?

Again, the idea is confused. One argument I have heard used by North American first nation people is that shamanism is a native skill and those who are not native and who practice or aspire to its teachings must therefore be exploiters, colonialists or 'shame-ons' rather than shamans.

But we are all 'native' to somewhere and unfortunately this argument falls over quickly for two reasons. Firstly, the very word shaman comes from the Tungus people of Siberia (it comes from the word *saman* which literally means 'a priest of the Altai people') not from North America, so those who make statements like this must by their own definition be exploiting native (Siberian) people by using a title that is not their own. Secondly, traditional healing practices are common to all cultures and no-one has a monopoly on them. The word shamanism has come into general usage to describe these practices precisely because the approach they take is essentially the same in all countries even though they arose independently of each other. North American tribes do not 'own' the sweatlodge for example; stone-built sweat houses can still be found in many parts of Ireland. Nor do they 'own' cleansings with herbs, as in smudging rituals; limpia (soul-cleaning with palo santo, agua florida and other plant essences) can be found in the Andes, in Haiti and Africa. We – all of us – have a shamanic past and modern practitioners are continuing a tradition which has existed for thousands of years because of the benefits it brings. There is nothing fake or plastic about it.

In my experience those Westerners who advance the 'plastic shaman' argument have turned out on further examination not only to be ill-informed, holding ideas and notions which they have not thought through, but at their core they are angry individuals who want *their* healings for free because of a right they feel they have. They may *want* this healing (and often sound as if they need it) but they have no more *right* to it than anyone else.

And of course as healers we have rights too. We do not *have* to take a client because they demand it from us. This feeling of entitlement in fact may be one of the issues that (if we do choose to accept them as clients) the healing will need to address.

In summary, it is my view that if prospective clients approach us with a genuine healing need and believe that we are the people to help them they will find a way to pay for what is on offer. That may sound harsh but I can only refer to myself in this and I know without doubt that if I was ill or in pain and I truly wanted help from someone who I knew in my heart could give it I would pay whatever it took.

In short then, you have a right to charge for your services and to set a fair price according to your assessment of what your skills are worth. No healer should feel pressurised to offer free healings because of the views of others.

Sex in Healing

There are horror stories (and you will no doubt come to hear them now you are starting to move in shamanic circles) about healers who have become involved with clients outside of the healing relationship. The issue often originates with the client but healers can be affected by it and need to know what they may be getting into.

There is a psychological concept in healing called transference. Basically, in a shamanic healing context it means that your client may come to regard you as a saviour, guru, the father they've never had or the understanding lover they've longed for but never known rather than the professional you are and the healer that he or she first came to see. Shamanically speaking it is a transfer of energy or power from the client to you and more common where the client visits you for more than one healing and a familiarity or implied friendship develops between you. Eventually he or she may come to see you as an object of affection or a potential lover instead of a healing professional. This is a natural process and in many ways it can't be avoided. It goes without saying, however, that the healer should act honourably and never take advantage of it.

Problems can arise for both healer and client when the healer not so much accepts what the client is projecting onto him or her but gives the client too much credit for acting in a responsible and adult fashion with regard to his or her emotions. That is, the healer may believe (or wish to believe) that the client knows what she is doing and is acting consciously and with awareness when she is affectionate towards him. If he is attracted to her as well he might feel that a romantic or sexual relationship could be possible between them. In another context it might be, but in the healing context it rarely ever is.

During any ensuing relationship the issue of power will likely remain and need to be addressed. In a healthy relationship, that is, most partners are equal but if one is giving power and control over their lives to another it can become destructive for them both. The client-partner ceases to take responsibility for his decisions and actions and the healer-partner comes to feel that she does not have a lover so much as an ongoing healing situation in which she has become an active (albeit unwilling) participant.

It can also be difficult to end relationships like this in a good way. There may still be problems, for example, because of all the client has projected onto you and by what may be made of this by him/her or by the people they tell and, in the worst-case scenario, by the legal profession.

One example is a healer who entered into a relationship with a student close to the end of a training course. She became pregnant, perhaps deliberately as it transpired, and then a few months later the relationship ended. She then began a campaign to discredit the healer for taking advantage of her even though the initial approach had been hers.

The golden rule then is this: do not become romantically or sexually entangled with a current client or student. When the healing relationship ends, if you are persuaded that a different sort of relationship may be possible, have a cooling off period where you will not see each other for a few weeks while you decide if you'd like to go ahead.

Talk honestly and openly to your one-time client as well and explain to them that you are not a guru but an individual like them and that, just as they have a job, healing is yours and there is no difference between you. Make sure they understand this and are not relying on you to be their healer forever and that they are prepared to play an equal part in the relationship.

This may sound incredibly unromantic but in these days of litigation and the desire to allocate 'blame' it may even be worth entering into a form of written agreement (like a pre-nup) before any other form of relationship begins and if he or she is not willing to do so, ask yourself honestly (and him or her) why not.

During healings, of course, you should also avoid any suggestion of sexual impropriety. A few students have asked me if it is necessary for the healer and/or client to remove their clothes during healings because some of the healers they had seen in the past had insisted on this. Commonsense should tell you NO. Emphatically NO. In shamanism we work with energy, the soul. If I can work with your energy body – the spirit that is within your physical self – to create beneficial change why should it matter that you are wearing jeans and a sweatshirt at the time?

In the notes I send to prospective clients before healings I even state that they will be lying down for their healing so women may wish to wear trousers rather than skirts. If during healings it seems likely that I will need to touch clients physically (for example, for spirit extraction procedures) I ask in advance if this is OK. If the client says no I simply don't put my hands on them and find another way to do the work – or else I just don't do it.

While checking out the energy flows in clients during a healing it might also be that there is a blockage at or near the genitals. This might be the case with clients who have been sexually abused in the past and it presents a special dilemma for healers since the normal procedure would be to work on this area as you would any other.

One approach to this, for the reasons above and to ensure that clients are at ease and relaxed, is not to go near these areas physically yourself but to find other ways of working energetically on them (for example by using stones or feathers to work through the energy body without needing to make direct contact) and/or to advise the client of the problem and suggest that he or she finds a specialist healer who can help. I appreciate that the latter is in some ways an opt-out but we are not in the business of distressing our clients – or of being sued – and there is a lot of room for confusion here.

Legal Issues

As well as the legal implications in what has been said above there are certain laws (current and forthcoming) which are relevant to what we may do and say as healers. Two of the most important have to do with mediumship and herbal prescriptions.

Ancient laws in the UK, for example, prevent anyone from advertising or carrying out services relating to mediumship, witchcraft or contacting the dead. Although these have not been invoked for years they are still on the statute books and are currently being reconsidered with a view to reviving or strengthening them. The result if they are reassessed is unlikely to be a 'witch hunt' on the scale we have seen before in history but they can still be used to bring charges. Equivalent laws no doubt exist in other European countries and US states and it is worth checking these. Practitioners should be wary therefore about promoting themselves with the use of 'inflammatory' terms which draw unwanted attention to the services they offer. 'Shamanic counselling' may be acceptable for example, but 'Mediumship and guidance from the dead' may not be.

Trading laws (such as the UK Trades Descriptions Act) may also be invoked if you over-claim or cannot prove that you are delivering what you offer. So, for example, you may be able to show that you did, in fact, provide client X with counselling services but it is less easy to prove that a deceased relative provided this counsel.

There are also plans to strengthen the laws about who may offer herbal prescriptions. In parts of Europe only qualified medical doctors may suggest herbs to clients or prepare potions for them and it looks as if other countries may also be going this way. If you work with plants and plant spirit medicines such legislation may impact you.

There may actually be some value in doctors being able to offer herbal cures – not least because pharmaceutical drugs often do more damage than good. A report in the London *Independent* newspaper [Jerome Burne, Turn Over a New Leaf, *The Independent*, May 10, 2005] revealed for example that:

The Medicines and Healthcare products Regulatory Agency (MHRA) – the government group responsible for regulating UK medicines including herbs – says that between 2000 and 2004 there were 451 reports of suspected adverse reactions involving herbal preparations of which 152 were serious. By way of comparison, consider this from a report in the *British Medical Journal* last year: 'In England alone [i.e. not including Scotland, Wales or Ireland] reactions to drugs that led to hospitalisation followed by death are estimated at 5,700 a year and could actually be closer to 10,000'. Herbs may not be completely safe as critics like to point out, but they are a lot safer than drugs.

There have also been some spectacular drug failures. In 2005 for example the FDA, after an extensive review of hundreds of studies, issued a warning that the use of antidepressants may actually lead to an *increase* in depression and suicidal thinking – the very outcomes these drugs are supposed to cure. The Yahoo news story that covered this warning noted the FDA's concerns that 'antidepressants may cause agitation, anxiety and hostility in a subset of patients who may be unusually prone to rare side effects... psychiatrists say there is a window period of risk just after pill use begins, before depression is really alleviated but when some patients experience more energy, perhaps enabling them to act on suicidal tendencies'. By contrast, the herbal cure for depression, St John's Wort, has never harmed anyone. As the *Independent* newspaper put it: '[St John's Wort] is not only more effective in the treatment of moderate to severe depression according to the *British Medical Journal*, but it also has fewer side-effects.'

The problem, however, is that medicine is a business as well as a rational science and by allowing only doctors to prescribe herbal treatments the impetus to do so, the intuition and the heart (the true healing) may be removed. In the words of the old saying: 'The operation was successful but the patient died'. There will also be many doctors who, although they can prescribe herbs, will choose not to because of their established preference for drugs (and the income this brings them from pharmaceutical companies) so we may see a decline in the use of natural medicines altogether.

In a sense the legal issues facing us are the same as they ever were. The witch hunts of a few hundred years ago, anthropologists argue, were instituted by the medical guilds which were forming at the time and looking for supremacy so they could protect their members and profits. To ensure this, traditional healers, 'wise women', 'cunning men' and the folk medicines and natural cures they provided could not be allowed to survive. The situation is similar today, with drug companies and medical professionals using the law to prevent herbal treatments by 'untrained' people and to counter the growing trend towards plant-based cures and natural medicines.

Practitioners therefore need to keep their eyes and ears open regarding these and other legal changes and to consider how they may be affected by them and what it may be safe for them to advertise.

When I make up herbal preparations for clients even now I add a statement to the effect that: 'For legal reasons I cannot make any claims regarding the effectiveness or otherwise of this mixture. The client uses it at his or her own risk and is advised to seek professional health care advice before using this preparation.' Clients understand the spirit in which this is done and are generally supportive but it is at least a safeguard in case of problems.

Insurance

There used to be a time when shamanism was so little known as a healing discipline that practitioners found it difficult to get insurance coverage. Things are changing but still there are not many insurance companies that actively promote coverage for shamanic healers. You will however find companies who are sympathetic to therapies such as reiki, aromatherapy, massage and so on and these are the companies to approach first.

You may be asked for evidence of your practice, your training and the length of time you have spent in either practical studies and/or working directly with clients so any proof of this you can collate (such as brochures, advertisements, leaflets, client endorsements and qualifications from your studies) will be useful. If you are a *Medicine for the Soul* graduate we will also provide a reference for you.

Professional practice cover will normally include:

- *Public Liability.* This protects you against liability to customers for injury or loss. For example, clients could trip and injure themselves while visiting your home or business premises.
- *Product Liability.* If as part of your healing work you sell or pass on any products to your customers, product liability provides you with cover against any liability arising out of the use of these.
- *Professional Indemnity.* This is insurance cover for advice you give to your clients and protects you in the event of any claims by the client as a result of alleged errors or omissions on your part which lead to loss or injury.
- *Libel and Slander.* If you write articles for trade journals or magazines this section of the insurance policy will cover you against any liability from this type of activity, for example if your article makes a point which another practitioner or client takes offence at or believes you are aiming your comments at them.

Once it was more a matter of choice for the practitioner whether he or she wished to invest in insurance or not, especially as it can be expensive (one shamanic organisation running courses and offering healings routinely spends more than £1,200 a year on insurance). It still is possible to explain to most clients the nature of shamanic work and (as in the case of herbal and other preparations above) to ensure that they understand that they undertake this work at their own risk and the majority of clients are fine with this. However, the UK is these days starting to become as litigious as its American neighbour, as evidenced by the frequency of daytime TV ads from no-win-no-fee legal companies who would like us all to believe that, 'Where's there's blame there's a claim' (forget about personal responsibility). I am sure that insurance will soon become a necessity rather than a luxury.

Quick Test 9

1. What healing tools should you prepare in advance of a client's arrival?
2. What can the breath tell you about the way your client might be feeling?
3. Suggest one piece of advice you might give a client after a healing.
4. How common is it in other cultures that shamans offer healing for free?
5. Suggest one possible danger of getting romantically involved with a client.
6. What legal issues have an impact on modern shamanism?

Exercises

Practice your journeying, dream work and work with omens. Please also undertake these next pieces of work.

1. Working with Clients

In your mind's eye recall any client you have worked with and, noting their posture, breathing, and remembering the things that were said and how, what other information did this give you in advance of the healing? Or now that the healing has been done, how does this additional information support your diagnosis and healing actions?

2. Issues

Would you ever offer healing free of charge to clients? Under what circumstances? Give two pros and two cons of doing so.

3. Finding a Code of Conduct

Bearing in mind some of the issues outlined in this chapter, journey to your guiding spirits and ask their advice on the conduct and approach you should take when working with clients. Record your journeys and from what you are told arrive at your own Code of Conduct which should have at least five points to it.

Quick Test Answers

Quick Test I

1. A shaman is a practitioner of the oldest psycho-spiritual tradition known to humankind. The word comes from the Tungus people of Siberia but now refers generally to someone who works with spiritual practices for healing, counselling or divination undertaken in partnership with Otherwordly guides, allies and helpers.

2. For example: plant spirit medicine, the use of aromas, massage, ritual, blessings, prayer, the use of sacred sound (drumming, chants, rattling, song), energy balancing and reiki-like techniques, soul retrieval, power return, spirit extraction and so on. Actually, just about any healing approach you can think of (including 'modern' skills of counselling and therapy and things we regard as recent inventions) can be traced back to a shamanic origin and are still in use today.

3. A shamanic journey is a means for the shaman to release his spirit so it can enter the Otherworlds to perform non-physical healing (bringing back power or soul fragments, etc, that have been lost by a client) and/or connect with his spirit guides for counselling, advice, information and support.

4. Ensure you are alone and undisturbed. Prepare your question (your reason for the journey) and express this as a clear intention. Make sure you have the necessary equipment to hand – your drum or drumming tape, for example, and a notebook and pen to record your observations.

5. Be clear in your intent and hold on to this throughout your journey. Make contact with your spirit allies and helpers before you do anything else. (Both of these are crucial!)

6. For example: Upper world: ethereal, light, airy, 'landscaped', human-like spirits, reached by ascent through a membrane-

like film between worlds. Middle world: a mythic or energetic parallel to our own world, a world of ideas and thoughtforms, discarnate spirits, a place that might be described as melancholy. Lower world: primal, earthy, less landscaped, animal spirits, elementals and ancestors, reached by descent.

Quick Test 2

1. In the Western world we are taught to seek the symbols of having 'made it' but these often disempower us in various ways. The new car or the executive home, while nice in itself, also means we must work to fund and maintain it. In doing so we give away some of our humanity and live someone else's dream of how life 'should' be. We can, of course, live any life we choose and explore our humanity in full but if we decide to live a life of convention by the rules of others then inevitably we must sacrifice something of ourselves in order to 'be in the game'.

2. A geis, in modern terms, is a script for our lives that has been given to us by another; usually a 'more powerful' person (for example, a parent). It is an implied pressure for us to behave in a certain way. This can become a habit for us as we either go along with or fight against this script. Either way it becomes a central concern of our lives so we do not live according to who we are (or could be) but, in one way or another, are engaged with someone else's definitions of us. In this way we sacrifice something of our being.

3. When we choose to forgive another we refuse to remain attached to a particular person or event and no longer give our power to it. Forgiveness, in shamanic terms, is an act not only (or even) of generosity and goodwill to another but a gesture of power for ourselves.

4. A Petty Tyrant is someone who pushes our buttons in a particular way, causing us to look at ourselves and see the things we would like to ignore or suppress but in fact need to

correct or change. For this reason don Juan saw them as 'worthy opponents' and advised Castaneda to seek out a tyrant for himself if one did not present naturally. When we have tyrants in our lives we also have a mirror to ourselves so we can use them as a source of knowledge. In this way they become allies for us not enemies, so we can take our power back and grow instead of giving it away to them.

Quick Test 3

1. Smudge can be used to cleanse and purify and is a traditional means of carrying prayers to the spirits for healings or blessings. It can also act as a useful diagnostic tool – if the smoke appears to be pushed away from the body or sucked in at certain points it can suggest that power has been lost from the energy body.

2. Chants, mantras and sacred songs can empower the soul or bring it home from where it is lost. As the shaman sings he guides participants in ceremony to places of healing in the Otherworlds. This is also a form of vibrational medicine, used to create physical changes. The Power Song is a magical tune, sometimes with clear and understandable words, sometimes in meta-language, given to a shaman by his power animals or allies to fill him with power or which he can sing into the body of a client to heal him.

3. Plants are a means of communion with the spirit worlds. They may speak to the shaman during his journey and recommend themselves for a client. Plants and their aromas can also be used for more magical uses, to change a person's luck, give them energy or draw love and success to them, as in the examples of Hoodoo oils.

Quick Test 4

1. Illness is caused by either a loss of power or the intrusion into our systems of an energy that is out of resonance with our

own. The former is known as power or soul loss. The latter is known as a spirit intrusion.

2. The energy body is a band of energy sometimes described as a 'luminous egg' (Castaneda) that surrounds and infuses us and gives us the power we draw from during our lives.

3. The ti bon anje (little good angel) is one of the three souls that, according to Haitian shamans, all humans have. It might be regarded as the most important of our souls since it is the one we use in our daily lives and the one most open to attack from energetic forces in the world that arise from moral failings or an unwillingness to take responsibility for our actions.

4. A spirit intrusion (also known as a power intrusion) is an energetic force from the unseen world that attaches itself to us and begins to eat away at our power, leaving us depleted and dis-spirited. Stress can be regarded as a modern example.

Quick Test 5

1. Spirit extraction is the removal of energies from a client that are not hers and do not serve her. It is performed by gazing the energy body and then journeying into the client's energy system and either negotiating with the spirit to leave (offering it a new home so it can do so) or by grabbing the entity and blowing it away to the safe-keeping of your Nature ally.

2. Power retrieval is the return of power to a client performed through journeying to a power animal that agrees to work with her and blowing it into her energy body.

3. Soul parts can leave because of:
   (a) The actions of the client and her guilt surrounding these. Confession can help.
   (b) The actions of another towards her and the trauma these cause. Soul retrieval by the healer is recommended.
   (c) Because of shock or fright. Working gently on the client's body to encourage the soul part to return home may be all that is needed.

4. Revise the framework for healing in this chapter.

Quick Test 6

1. Shamanic counselling is a journey where the shaman speaks out the visions that he sees and the information he receives so that a client can hear it and be guided by the symbols, metaphors or direct advice that comes from spirit. Some shamans record on tape the journey they are taking as it unfolds so the client can refer to it later. A drumming tape is normally used.

2. Shamanic core process is where a shaman guides the client on her own journey, using drum and voice to gently direct her through the stages of entry to the lower world to meet her spirit allies and find answers to her questions. For clarity the journey is done in stages with the shaman drumming for the client and guiding her in words.

3. There are many types of divination. Three examples are:

   - *Threshold divination:* Hold the client's question in mind and then find three places that represent thresholds or boundaries. Close your eyes and turn three times then open them and make a note of the first thing you see. When this is done write all three things down and create a story from them that answers the client's question.
   - *Rock divination:* Allow yourself to be called to a rock that attracts you and look at it from four sides. Make a note of the things you see there. Then use your imagination to create a story that includes them all and which has a relationship to your client's question.
   - *Journeying to a future self:* Journey in the normal way to a possible future for your client based on the outcome of a decision she needs to make. Bring this information back to your client (or talk it aloud) for discussion.

Quick Test 7

1. A psychopomp is a conductor of souls – a shaman working with the spirits of the dead to heal or release them from a sorrowful attachment to the Earth. This requires a middle world journey and negotiation with the spirit concerned before the shaman opens the doorway to the spiritual dimension so this entity can be reunited with its ancestors and loved ones in spirit.

2. The near-death archetype is similar to the soul flight of the shaman in the following ways:

   - A sensation of being out-of-body, rising up and floating above the physical self
   - A sensation of rushing quickly through a dark tunnel towards a source of light or being lifted up and looking back to the Earth
   - A meeting with wise and loving spirits; consultation with these spirits
   Information received from them in the form of a life review or 'karmic learning'
   - Sometimes a reluctance to come back

3. Spirits of place are the natural spirits or energies of any environment. To the shaman all things are alive. These spirits can be consulted to find out how improvements can be made to this place to benefit the humans (and the spirits) who live there.

4. Feng shui is a modern form of ancient shamanic techniques which work with energy flows and Earth medicine. It teaches that we can empower certain areas of buildings to enhance or improve their energies. Three feng shui tools are crystals, wind chimes and mirrors to deflect or recirculate energy.

5. One way of purifying a house is to walk the rooms and smudge them. In New Orleans a mix of basil, eucalyptus

leaves and myrrh is used but a sage stick will work just as well.

Quick Test 8

1. Ayahuasca – the vine of souls – is a visionary plant used ritually in the Amazon for opening the doors of perception and bringing guidance about life purpose and information on the nature of the spiritual universe.

2. Teacher plants are sacred plants used in visionary rituals that offer profound insights into the nature of life and reality. They are distinguished from other plants because they are a consciousness with a much wider purpose than medicine plants which may have only a single healing intention.

3. The plant diet is a way of communing with the spirit of a plant by eating only bland food and abstaining from certain activities that might take the mind off the plant itself. This focus ensures a much deeper connection with its spirit.

4. The medsen fey is a leaf doctor – shaman and master herbalist – of Haiti. Medsen fey receive healing information from their Lwa (spirit guides) or from the spirit of the plants themselves who appear to them in dreams.

Quick Test 9

1. A blanket and pillows for your client to lie down on, smudge mix or incense and a holder for this, a lighter or matches for the smudge and candles, your rattle and your drum and/or drumming tape. Optionally also (depending on how you work and the affinity you have for certain tools over others) a selection of feathers (and/or an egg) in case extraction is necessary, at least four quartz crystals, a pendulum and a collection of stones (for energy rebalancing and mapping the energy body).

2. For example, breathing high up in her chest may suggest fear as she talks of a particular issue (fear probably means an issue

to do with power loss); low in her stomach may suggest grief (and this might imply the need for a releasing ritual).

3. You might suggest for example that your client leaves it a few weeks for her energies to settle before she makes any major life changes and that she is as gentle and forgiving with herself as she can be during this time. She should also drink plenty of water to assist her new energies to flow, get as much sleep as she needs and take time out in nature. And of course she should follow the guidance of spirit if any counselling information has been passed to her, as long as she feels it is safe and appropriate for her to do so.

4. Shamans in other cultures rarely if ever offer healings free of charge. They may, however, take payment in non-monetary forms such as food or services.

5. There are several potential problems (including getting sued). The biggest single danger and cause of these problems is the transference of power from client to healer.

6. The legal situation with regard to healing is changing all the time. Two current issues have to do with herbal prescriptions and who may give them and what can be said or claimed about the healing itself, which will have an impact on how you advertise your services and conduct yourself with clients.

Your Shamanic Qualification

Your study of shamanic healing is concluded – for now, although as a healer you will always be learning. You have *initiated* into shamanism (to initiate anything is to begin it) but the journey continues and this is its pleasure and excitement.

You have come a long way and now know many secrets of the shaman: how shamanic healing is done, how energies are rebalanced, power and soul returned and how negative energies are removed from the body, the home and the environment. You have everything you need to begin shamanic healings of your own and if you have followed this course as suggested you will also have practical experience in these areas. The Four Gates Foundation now offers you an opportunity to have your skills recognised through the award of a Diploma in Shamanic Studies.

For those serious about developing their abilities as healers the Diploma means that you can receive feedback and suggestions about the exercises you have completed in this book and the practical work you have done. Through this you can also hone your healing skills.

Another benefit if you want to work as a healer is the confidence it gives clients who can see from your qualification that you have the experience you claim and that this has been assessed and validated by an independent organisation. If you are a therapist working in other areas of healing your Diploma might also be used as evidence of Continual Professional Development (CPD). (Check with your tutor on this.) Finally, you may also receive client referrals from us.

We are frequently contacted by clients who are looking for a shamanic practitioner in their area. We send them the list of healers who have trained with us and they are able to contact them directly. This provides them with the healing they need and an income for healers (we take no commission). Some graduates have been able to start a new career as healers, gaining clients of their own based on initial referrals from us.

If you'd like to proceed in this way let me know and I'll tell you how. Otherwise, I wish you great luck for the future. You have the skills now to work on your own healing and that of others – skills much needed in this world of challenges and change. Blessings on your path.

Ross Heaven
Montefrio, Spain and Newhaven, England
2011
Email: ross@thefourgates.org
Web: www.thefourgates.org

About The Author

Ross Heaven, the founder and director of The Four Gates Foundation, is the author of several books on shamanism and healing and runs workshops on these themes in Europe and Peru, including Shamanic Practitioner training programmes, Shamanic Healing and Soul Retrieval, plant medicine retreats and journeys to Peru to work with indigenous shamans. He is also a shamanic healer and therapist and offers counselling and healing in the UK.

He has a website at www.thefourgates.org where you can read more about his work as well as forthcoming books and other items of interest. He also provides a monthly newsletter update by email which you can receive free of charge by emailing ross@thefourgates.org.

His full book list can be viewed at Amazon Books.

Moon Books, invites you to begin or deepen your encounter with Paganism, in all its rich, creative, flourishing forms.